*Chaos, Wonder and the
Spiritual Adventure of Parenting*

Chaos, Wonder and the Spiritual Adventure of Parenting

An Anthology

Sarah Conover and Tracy Springberry, Editors

Skinner House Books
Boston

Printed in the United States

Cover and text design by Suzanne Morgan

print ISBN: 978-1-55896-615-4
eBook ISBN: 978-1-55896-616-1

6 5 4 3 2 1
14 13 12 11

Publication credits and copyright acknowledgments are on page 242.

Library of Congress Cataloging-in-Publication Data

Chaos, wonder and the spiritual adventure of parenting : an anthology /
Sarah Conover and Tracy Springberry, editors.
     p. cm.
   Rev. ed.; previously published under title: At work in life's garden.
   Includes bibliographical references.
   ISBN 978-1-55896-615-4 (pbk. : alk. paper) – ISBN 978-1-55896-616-1
(ebook)
   1. Parenting. 2. Parent and child. I. Conover, Sarah. II.
Springberry, Tracy. III. At work in life's garden.
   HQ755.8.C65455 2011
   204'.41–dc22
                                        2010053876

For Karen Gagney, a remarkable parent to many, and for the dear friends who helped to parent my children.
Indeed, it takes a village.

—SARAH CONOVER

For my children Mercury, Nashua, Solomon, and Ella, who taught me the meaning of unconditional love.

—TRACY SPRINGBERRY

care

Sarah Conover and Tracy Springberry are proud to donate four percent of the royalties from sales of this book to CARE, a leading humanitarian organization fighting global poverty.

Contents

Embracing Life

Introduction

When parents-to-be tell us they plan to keep their current lives intact when their baby is born, we both laugh. We laugh because that's what we thought too. We believed that somehow, after we'd had a baby, the basic structure of our lives would be the same, and that we'd be the same people with the same interests, desires, hopes, and dreams.

Instead, the birth of each of our children changed us forever by opening us—sometimes gently, sometimes painfully—to wonder, love, and life. At first, we didn't think this had anything to with spirituality or wisdom. Why would we? The stories our culture tells about the spiritual journey imply that children clutter this quest. Children fill lives with noise, mess, and demands. Their parents can't focus on the quiet contemplation that will bring them closer to themselves, to mystery, or to the holy. The most spiritual people, we've been told, don't have children to take care of. The Buddha left his wife and son when be became a seeker. Jesus did not have children, nor did Mother Theresa or the Dalai Lama. In both the East and West, we believe that the truly spiritual give their lives to God in monasteries or nunneries.

So Sarah deepened her spiritual life through Buddhist practice, and Tracy found a spiritual path by studying for the Unitarian Universalist ministry. Then at some point, as we stumbled through parenting—learning, day after day, to love unconditionally, to forgive, to be present when we didn't want to be, and to simply sit in awe of life—we realized that the idea that children clutter the spiritual quest was simply wrong. Instead, having a child throws us, whether we are willing or not, whether we recognize it or not, onto the path toward spiritual wisdom. We pass through an initiation and can never go back. We can't wake up and change our minds.

In the context of parenting, the spiritual—that maddening, slippery, vague idea defined at best by tautologies—becomes tangible. It is felt, touched, and communicated daily as the tone and color of family life. We hear, taste, breathe, and touch the spiritual through the ways we attend, together, to countless sunrises, meals at the family table, celebrations, frustrations, grief, joys, laughter, and responsibilities. We feel its press in the disparity between the path we hope to walk—full of kindness, love, forgiveness—and the path we actually walk.

The essays in this book offer testimony to the ways parenting transforms parents. Writers tell how the chaos, the wonder, and the pain of raising children helped them engage more deeply with life. The essays are not from any specific spiritual or religious tradition. Some writers are practicing Unitarian Universalists, Catholics, or Buddhists, while others claim no particular religious or spiritual affiliation.

We organized our material around three themes. In the first section, "Waking," writers explore those times when children help us see the mystery and beauty of life: a toddler beams a smile and the parent basks in the blessing of unconditional love; a parent holds a sick child and understands completely just how both fragile and resilient life is; a child experiences something new, helping the parent see it for the first time. In this section, Alexandra Fuller shares her unexpected, overwhelming love for her newborn daughter; Scott Russell Sanders discovers that hope for the future is a gift he must give his son and himself; and Beth Kephart sees beauty when she only expects to see brokenness.

In the second section, "Struggles with Love," essays describe the ways children throw us into battles of the heart. "If you really want a tour of your own dark impulses," write the authors of *Raising Cain*, a book about parenting boys, "have children; it will put you in touch with all of your most uncontrolled and regrettable impulses." This fact is set against another truth: Having children makes us want to love perfectly. The tension between these truths causes anguish, but forces growth. My four-year-old hurls a glass of juice across the room, screaming, "I want milk!" In a flash of anger, I want to hit him. His survival and mine demand that I learn the critical spiritual skills of forgiveness, letting go, acceptance, and surrender to life as it is. In this section, Anne Lamott deals with losing her temper at her son; Nancy Mairs grapples with the idea that love is not always romantic or affectionate but a difficult form of being present; and Barbara Kingsolver learns that by loving and honoring herself she can love her daughter more fully.

The third section, "Embracing Life," explores how children help us say yes to living, even when we feel cynical and angry about the future, or when life feels painful because of death, illness, or family turmoil. These essays consider how raising children can launch parents on faith journeys and commitments to justice. Here Jess Walters realizes that, for him, gratitude and salvation is in the relationships with the people he loves; Brian Doyle discovers hope in the young and the old, and Rosemary Bray McNatt finds that that the birth of her children propelled her into a life of service.

In his poem, "Words for my Daughter," John Balaban describes his daughter as "sent to call me back into our helpless tribe." Children call us back to love, to suffer, and to grow in ways we could not have anticipated. Their presence insists that we journey the spiritual path, embracing the world from a depth and breadth that we could not imagine before we began. Balaban's words, as well as the essays within this anthology, continue to alert us that we are full-fledged members of a helpless tribe, called back time and again by the children.

Yet isn't every human being, parent or not, a member of this tribe? As Noelle Oxenhandler says in her essay, "Boundary Loss,"

"Everyone is either the child of a parent or the parent of a child or both … as if everyone were at least a double image, everyone pregnant, in a sense, with someone else." The treasure that the writers here give us is the reminder that perhaps we can't know who we really are, or what the holy really is, without each other.

Waking

"…but still it is a mystery, it is beyond human, how these two children in their crumple of bones glide and circle each other and spin, their wheels making no noises as they turn, their faces shy, soft as feathers, and triumphant."

— BETH KEPHART

Alexandra Fuller

Life

The rainy season leaked on through March by which time I had forgotten what it felt like to live without nausea and exhaustion. For hours at a time, I watched rain cry down the windows in the bedroom. Heat and humidity settled like breath somewhere north of my stomach. I began to have fantasies about strawberries and snow and chocolate breakfast cereal none of which were available but which all seemed to promise a reprieve from my condition.

At weekday lunchtimes, the *mazungu* doctor in Lusaka was usually to be found drinking deeply of South African wine at the Marco Polo restaurant, indifferent to the constraints of the conventional lunch hour. He didn't bother to remove his white clinical coat or his stethoscope when leaving his offices at noon. This being Zambia, a medical emergency could arise at any moment. Surgery using knife and fork and red wine.

He was the acknowledged authority on malaria, bilharzia and rabies, and though he couldn't treat you, he would tell you—without frills—if you were among the one-in-three Zambians to have acquired HIV. He carelessly dispensed the few medications available to him for the treatment of dysentery, tuberculosis, ringworm, giardia, syphilis, witchcraft, kwashiorkor and tick fever. But he did not consider the possibility of pregnancy a medical condition.

For the third time in three months, the pregnancy test administered by the doctor's nurse had come back without a red stripe in the right-hand window. "Are you sure the tests aren't out of date? Perhaps they've expired." I cleared my throat and the doctor looked at his watch again. I was making him late for his customary bottle of South African wine. I thought about how else I might phrase this and at last I say, "You may want to just have a quick peek up there. Just to make sure."

"A peek?" said the doctor with distaste.

"A little peek," I tried.

Which he wouldn't do. Especially before lunch.

"You have an IUD installed, no?"

"Well, yes."

"So?"

So, for the third time in as many months he declared my pregnancy hysterical and for the third time in as many months I waved my gratitude and farewell at him, mouth covered, and hurried off to the clinic loos where I vomited noisily and prolifically to the distress of patients waiting for their prescriptions at the pharmacy.

"I must have a tummy bug after all," I told Charlie.

But then the hard lump of baby in my belly became impossible to deny. And I must have been throwing up for a reason.

If it wasn't cholera. Which it wasn't.

And if I hadn't had my period for three months, which I hadn't.

Dad, up from the farm, said, "Well of course you're in-calf."

"But the pregnancy tests came back negative."

"Tests? *Pah.*"

"Damn."

Dad lit a cigarette. "Don't worry. Half of all heifers lose their first take."

"No, it's not that," I said. "No, Dad. I want the baby."

"Oh." He was embarrassed and didn't know what to say. He stirred more sugar into his tea. "Well, then…." Dad was trying, in his rough way, to protect me from what he thought I don't know. "*Ja*, well, don't be disappointed, that's all. You know, if.... It's common to have a practice run."

I didn't have the heart to tell him that I had already had a practice run.

Years ago I took care of that. On an anonymous, thin, plastic-sheeted bed, a stranger's white-gloved hands in a Canadian hospital took care of that. I don't tell Dad that I cried for days into a friend's pillow and smoked all my friend's cigarettes and bled into his toilet until he came and carried me, inexpertly, to bed, and let me bleed onto his sheets. He was not the father of the child I had chosen to lose, just an old friend with a car and a basement apartment near campus and a big heart.

The old friend had said (holding me), "I had a hamster I really loved when I was a kid. And one day I hugged the little fucker to death, by mistake." He stroked my head, "So I know how you feel." Then we put a towel under me, and he said, "Shit, how much blood is there to lose?" My friend said, "You need fluids," and fetched me a cold beer.

I told Dad that there were worse things than finding out you're pregnant.

We decided we should drive through the border at Chirundu and up to Harare, Zimbabwe, for the advice of a medical expert. We had to stop periodically so I could throw up: after the winding Zambezi escarpment and at the urine-smelling border post and behind the diesel-belching buses at Cloud's End.

The Zimbabwean gynecologist confirmed via ultrasound that I was pregnant. He showed me where the baby lay, a little pulse in my womb. I looked up at the pictures on the doctor's wall describing fetal development, and I imagine my baby, her tiny fists curled in a Black Power salute ("*Free Nelson Mandela! Send him home to So-wet-oh*") and then the doctor showed me where the intrauterine device may hinder her growth.

"If you leave the IUD *in situ*, you risk losing the baby. Or worse."

"What can be worse?"

The doctor shrugged, an African educated in London, with the schooling of the west, but his own people's matter-of-factness about life, death, loss, "It's for you to decide. Perhaps some… impediment to growth."

"And if I have the IUD removed?"

"You still risk losing the baby."

I stared up at the wall, at the little defiant fist on the smudgy black-and-white photograph of someone else's baby. I said, "I don't think I'll lose this one."

Then I offered my arm to the clinic's nurse and blood was siphoned off. I am tested for HIV/AIDS, syphilis, gonorrhea.

Charlie had gone outside to the car, and I went out to look for him. There were other potential fathers kicking their heels in the dust and smoking cigarettes, leaning up against farm pickups while their pregnant wives were inside the whitewashed walls of the clinic.

"Well, I'm definitely pregnant." I crossed my arms and looked away so Charlie couldn't see my tears, and I said, "Bugger, bugger, bugger. He says I might lose it."

Charlie reached out for me again; and this time I let him rock me against his shoulder. And then morning sickness took over, and I fought my way out of his embrace to throw up in the gynecologist's beautiful orange cannas.

We chose a small clinic in a village east of Harare to have the IUD removed. I didn't want to lose the baby, but if I did, I wanted to bury her somewhere I would find her again. Somewhere small and quiet and where I could come back and find the flowers I'd planted for her.

I was bedded next to an old-timer in a tiny ward for two that overlooked a pine forest and a comforting, bright new garden of English-country-garden flowers; lavender, nasturtiums, rhododendrons, and roses.

"What you here for?" asked my neighbor, patting her covers happily and eyeing me over the top of her glasses.

"I'm pregnant," I said.

"Well, you don't look it," she said suspiciously.

"That's because I'm not very far along."

"Good, then we won't have any squawking kids in here any time soon."

"No."

The old lady had been prescribed sherry before lunch, "to stimulate my appetite," she explained. "I can tell you something else, I haven't had so much fun…." She sipped her sherry appreciatively. "Underestimated for the digestion," she confided. Then added, "I can't stand babies." She offered me a sip from her glass, which I declined weakly, nauseated. "They won't let me smoke though."

"Oh."

"Call me old-fashioned, but I don't have a problem with smoking. Do you? You wouldn't mind if I smoked, would you?"

I grunted.

The pre-op drugs were starting to take effect. My mouth was dry, and my legs felt as if they were floating.

"I hate visiting day," said my neighbor with sudden vehemence. "They all come to see me and sit on my bed and I can't read. I can't knit. And they're so boring."

"Who?" I asked feebly.

"My children. Their children. The whole bloody lot of them. They *whinge*."

The last thing I heard and saw before they wheeled me into the operating room was the old lady, raising her sherry glass in salute and asking loudly, urgently, "From what? You didn't say from what? What are you pregnant from?" and looking around the place as if expecting an attack from an unknown quarter.

Charlie was there when I woke up. For a man not given to emotion, he looked close to tears, "It's going to be okay."

"I'm still pregnant?"

"So far. They're going to give you something to help you sleep.

I'll come get you tomorrow."

I drifted in and out for the next twelve hours, unable to struggle out of the deep, drugged sleep completely, even as I fought it. During the night, a long, green snake found its way into our ward. My old neighbor, assisted by a man whom I vaguely remember as being attached by a pole to an intravenous drip, killed it with a walking stick and draped it on the end of a broom handle.

It had only been a poor, fat house snake.

The doctor told me to take it easy for the next few days.

"Any idea when she's due?" I asked.

"How do you know it's a she?"

I shrugged. "Just do," I replied.

The doctor sighed and pressed her hands to my belly, "You're three months along, I'd say." She shut her eyes and felt along the ridges of my ribs, "The end of August," she announced, "maybe early September."

We came back in late August to wait for the baby. We stayed in the highlands for a fortnight, hiking in the relief of cool, pine-scented air, and then the doctor decided there was no more room for the baby to be in my great swinging belly; it was time for us to persuade her to come out.

The local vicar's wife was found to have the same blood group as mine and was told to stand by for a couple of days (veins at the ready) in case I should need her blood. A seventy-year-old tennis-playing farmer's wife who had, forty years earlier, delivered twins (vaginally and without medical intervention or pain relief) was summoned to give me a few pointers on the birthing process. She kept her lesson brief (swinging her tennis racquet around experimentally all the time), "Piece of old tackie, really," she said, sending an imaginary lob over my shoulder. "Women have been doing this since Adam and Eve, so just remember—you're not doing anything special." (Slam!) "Just keep breathing, don't bother with the hollering, and you'll be fine."

"Thank you."

She turned to Charlie, "I've rafted the Zambezi," she announced, twisting to execute an air-backhand. "That's what childbirth is like," she informed me unhelpfully, "wave after wave. Wa-boom! And then you hit an eddy."

"I see."

"An enema will really help get this labor going," the Shona midwife told me. I am already pinned to the bed with pain and, as far as I have been told, we're not even close to a cigar. The midwife looms in and out of my range of vision, which is mostly the pale blue tent made by the blanket hung between my knees and a high barred window that is leaking in a pale, spring light.

"A what?"

"Come on," she said, producing a length of thin red hosepipe, "roll over on your side."

"Oh my God, no, you're not going to…"

Mum, who had driven down with us from Zambia to help me deliver the baby grinned unhelpfully.

"Mu-um!"

She said, "I heard of a movie star that got a gerbil stuck in his bottom once. Just think about that. That's got to be worse than an enema."

"Out," I said, glaring at Mum and Charlie, "both of you out!" I groaned through a contraction.

"Keep an eye out for gerbils, ha, ha."

"Not funny, Mum."

The door slammed behind my mother and husband.

"And stay there," I shouted, " 'til I tell you."

The midwife said, "This is a good remedy for a slow labor."

"It's humiliating is what it is." (I had imagined a placid labor, set to gentle music while I smiled bravely through the pain and effortlessly produced a perfect baby.)

She laughed, "Humiliating? My dear, a day from now you will know what true humiliation is."

"Oh God," I held onto the edge of the bed and gritted my teeth.

By four o'clock in the afternoon the baby had been stuck for hours. The doctor put the kettle on. "Keep pushing," she told me, "and you'll get this baby out in time for tea." Now that anything I have to say has been reduced to words of one syllable, Mum and Charlie have been called back into the room. I grabbed Mum's arm on one side and the midwife's arm on the other, dug my chin into my chest and pushed. Charlie peered hopefully at my bottom.

"Nope," he announced.

I came up for air, "Fuck off. Please."

Charlie got out of range.

Now the kettle was boiling. The doctor scooped tea leaves into a pot and poured hot water over them, the steamy, sweet smell of brewing tea added to the close, sweaty atmosphere in the room.

I dug my nails into Mum's hand, "I don't think I can do this," but then another contraction came and I pushed into the endless, deep pain of it.

The doctor glanced at the teapot ruefully, "Time to get this baby out," she told me, rolling up her sleeves. She brought out a knife and something that looked like a toilet plunger. I shut my eyes.

"Just keep breathing," said Charlie reemerging from his corner.

"Fuck off."

Mum held onto my shoulders and the midwife held onto my legs (like a cow, I thought), and the doctor pulled. If she'd brought out a rope and chain and pulled the child out with the help of a tractor, I would not have been surprised.

I thought of the men at the dip pulling a difficult calf from a cow, singing as they heaved, "*Potsi, piri, tatu, ini.*"

Somewhere far away, somewhere else in the hospital, I heard a woman scream.

Mum said, "Shhhhh." And I realized the scream had come from me.

"Push," said the Shona midwife.

I pushed, the doctor pulled, and Mum held on.

Then the baby was on my stomach and I was crying. She was long-limbed, dark-haired, blood-smeared, and perfect. She had lips like rosebuds. I put my arms over her and I knew, suddenly and unexpectedly, that I had been put on this earth for one reason only: to give life to this child.

"Cup of tea?" asked the midwife, propping a cup next to me on the bed.

"That'll do you good," said Mum, "put a bit of sugar in it."

"I hate sugar in my tea."

At a basin in the corner of the ward, a fourteen-year-old girl who had come into the clinic hours after me was preparing to leave. She was up, fully dressed, and was bathing and dressing her new baby. If she can do it, I can do it, I thought. I felt for the edge of my bed and swung my feet onto the floor. Supporting myself against the bed frame, I had a brief vision of the young girl's face and her pink-clothed baby. Then a swimming and indistinct sense that the floor was slipping away from me and rolling up to become the ceiling. Blackness rushed into my head and I was on the floor.

Mum fetched a basin of water and a bar of soap, "I'll give you a bed bath," she said, "you can try getting up tomorrow." The nurse came through to see how I was getting on and gave me a little white pill to help with the pain. As I drifted out of my mind in a comfortably drugged state I asked, slurring a little, "What's the pill?"

"Valium," said the nurse, drawing the curtains, "we find most … ladies need a little something to calm them after birth."

I sighed and sank back against the pillows. "The baby?" I asked, indistinctly.

"She's fine," someone murmured.

I heard Mum say to Charlie, "Ready for something a bit stiffer than tea?"

Charlie leant over me and planted a kiss on my forehead. A cigar leered out of his top pocket. "Well done, babe."

It wasn't until much later, in the middle of the night, that I struggled out of my fog and lay breathing into the darkness trying to remember where I was. Why did I feel as if I'd been torn in half? Jesus Christ! The baby! Where did I put the baby! I patted the bed next to me and groped wildly around the bedclothes. "Nurse!" No one came. I swung out of bed and hurried (clutching my bottom which felt as if it might slip out onto the floor) toward a mild light at the end of a dark passage.

"Is the baby here?"

The nurse on duty smelled of cigarettes and coffee. She was knitting, her feet comfortably propped up on the desk in front of her. "What are you doing out of bed, sweetie?"

"I'm looking for my baby."

"You can't have her until morning."

"It is morning," I said, letting myself behind the desk and looking around fighting the panic that had swelled in my chest. "Where did you put her?"

"It's okay darling. You go back and sleep. It's the last bit of shut-eye you'll be getting for a while."

"Where is she?" I insisted, planting myself firmly in front of the nurse and holding myself together. I'd seen a cow with a prolapsed uterus on the farm once.

The nurse counted her stitches and put her knitting down reluctantly.

"Come."

The baby was alone in a plastic box, with a bright light bulb hanging over her. "The light keeps her warm," said the nurse. Like baby chickens.

I scooped up the swaddled infant from the basin.

"I promise we can keep her here for you. I've been feeding her sugared water." The nurse sounded defensive, a little offended.

"It's alright," I said. "I'll take her now."

I held the soft sleeping thing up to my face and inhaled the fresh breath of her new lungs, the soft-kitten-blood smell of her recent birth.

I went back to bed, undressed myself and unrolled the baby, holding her next to my skin. She nestled into my breast, her rosebud mouth opened and closed over my nipple. I shut my eyes and closed my arms around her. "I promise I won't let you go," I told the baby. We fell asleep like that, both us naked, with her mouth soft and wet over my nipple and her breathing warm and steady against my neck.

Noelle Oxenhandler

Boundary Loss

Toward the end of my pregnancy, I found myself in the grip of a strange compulsion. Though the day was hot and my belly huge, I heaved myself the six long blocks to the public library and came home with a pile of books on the Middle East. In those last two weeks before the birth, even as I experienced the signs of imminent labor—the waves of tightening in the abdomen, the mix of acute cellular vigilance and overwhelming drowsiness, the impossibility of getting comfortable on any surface, in any position whatsoever—I ate and slept and read about Lebanon, Israel, Jordan, the Palestinians, about borders, ethnic hatreds, civil wars....

Only a short while before my reading binge, I'd been immersed in an irresistible and very classic form of nesting. With manic intensity, I'd painted a great many things in my house—walls, sills, chairs, a toy box, a lamp—a rosy peach the color of women's thighs and babies' rumps by Rubens. But what had come over me now could only be described as anti-nesting. I read with a mysterious, and even desperate necessity, making charts of the various factions and tragic milestones, the assassinations, the hostage-takings, the coups and bombings. If anyone had asked me "Why?" I would have told them, "Because it's my last chance in a long time to understand the world."

Then my daughter was born, and all the factions fell away. She was all there was. As she slept beside me the morning after her birth, I leaned out of my hospital bed to pull the plug out of a socket, and in that moment, I felt a rush of sadness for the socket. For in that moment the socket was a mouth and the plug was a nipple, everything in the world was either a mouth or a nipple, hunger or food, need or fulfillment.

In the days that followed, my field of vision gradually expanded around the small circle of mouth and milk. For a few days, everyone I saw was either a head or an opening that had made way for a head. If I saw a tall, distinguished-looking man talking on the television in elegant and lightly accented English about the NATO alliance, I would think to myself "What a large head he has," and a wave of feeling would move through me for his mother, whom I could see as though she were there before my eyes: a young girl lying on a cot in a hallway in Amsterdam, in 1944 or so, bombs falling in the city around her, their sound obliterated as someone with their hand on her sweating forehead says to her, "*Drukken!*" ("Push!").

From head and opening, my circle of vision grew to encompass mother and child, then parent and child, and I was struck by what seemed to me the blinding truth, a truth I'd never seen before, that *everyone is either the child of a parent or the parent of a child, or both.* I experienced this not as an idea but as an immediate perception so that I could not look at an individual human being without perceiving at the same time a parent or a child, as if everyone were at least a double image, everyone pregnant, in a sense, with someone else.

From this vantage point, violence and war were not even wrong, they were simply impossible, absurd. For the value of a single human life was not an abstract concept; it was the most tangible reality, a reality borne in my own flesh and as apparent to the naked eye as the color of a person's hair or skin, or the size and shape of his body.

This vision—with its utter clarity and simplicity—happened to crystallize for me from up close, in a condition of extreme nearness, at the moment I reached to pull a plug from a socket. But it is identical in essence to visions that others have had from a vast distance. When the astronaut Russell Schweickart was spinning in outer space, he saw our small blue planet floating in its vast sea of darkness, and saw simultaneously the fragility and the preciousness of the earth and all its inhabitants:

> The contrast between that bright blue and white Christmas-tree ornament and the black sky, that infinite universe, and the size and significance of it really comes through. It is so small and so fragile, such a precious little spot in the universe, that you can block it out with your thumb. You realize that everything that means anything to you—all of history and art and death and birth and love, tears and joys, all of it, is on that little blue-and-white spot out there which you can cover with your thumb.

The intensity of such visions fades. The spaceship returns to earth; the mother comes home from the hospital with her baby; and mundane life with its mix of fatigue, irritability, exhilaration, and blank space resumes. It is necessary that the intensity of such visions should fade; it is hard to navigate the sphere of daily life if one has difficulty pulling a plug from a socket. Even the Jains—wearing masks over their mouths and clearing a path through the grass where they walk so as not to inhale or trample insects—have to admit that some destruction, some callousness, is necessary in order to survive.

In 1926, Virginia Woolf recorded in her diary:

> Two resolute, sunburnt, dusty girls in jerseys and short skirts, with packs on their backs, city clerks or secretaries, tramping along the road in the hot sunshine of Ripe. My instinct at once throws up a screen, which condemns them: I think them in every way angular, awkward, and self-assertive. But all this is a great mistake. These screens shut me out....The screen-making habit, though, is so universal that probably it preserves our sanity. If we had not

this device for shutting people off from our sympathies, we might dissolve utterly; separateness would be impossible.

We might dissolve utterly, she writes. Once, during supper at a meditation retreat, I experienced such intense identification with the mouths of the faces opening and closing around me that I almost forgot to feed myself. Except for the awareness of dissolving, which remained, I felt myself dissolve utterly. There was great joy in that moment, and the sense of seeing directly into the face of who it is we really are, without screens. I would have liked to remain inside that moment, but I couldn't. It passed into another moment; I told myself "I'd better eat or I'll be hungry later," and I finished my soup, washed my bowl and silverware, and returned to the place that had my name on it in the meditation hall.

At that time, I wasn't yet a mother, but the moment was similar to the moment of pulling the plug from the socket, that moment when the whole world became a child's mouth and a mother's breast. There is something at the heart of the eros of parenthood that is truly radical—radical in its literal sense of root, and radical in the sense of its potentially transforming power. What if we were to tap the power of the boundary loss that lies at the root of each of us? The vision fades, the screens return, but it remains true that *everyone is either the child of a parent or the parent of a child or both*. Even the most unwanted child was once held by his mother's body, which made itself over for him. And for at least a moment, as he emerged from her body, her own being broke open to give birth to him, and he filled the whole world.

Two sunburnt, dusty girls tramp along a summer road. Virginia's eyes narrow and she sees them as *other*—and in their otherness, as angular, awkward, self-assertive. Then, for a moment, the screens fall away. The door that "shut(s) people off from our sympathies" opens, and the boundaries dissolve. Her eyes widen, darkening with kindness, and for a moment, she sees these two human beings in that other way, the way a mother or a father, eyes widening, sees the baby who burst through the opening they made in their lives.

Scott Russell Sanders

Mountain Music I

On a June morning high in the Rocky Mountains of Colorado, snowy peaks rose before me like the promise of a world without grief. A creek brimful of meltwater roiled along to my left, and to my right an aspen grove shimmered with new leaves. Bluebirds darted in and out of holes in the aspen trunks, and butterflies flickered beside every puddle, tasting the succulent mud. Sun glazed the new grass and licked a silver sheen along the boughs of pines.

With all of this to look at, I gazed instead at my son's broad back as he stalked away from me up the trail. Sweat had darkened his gray T-shirt in patches the color of bruises. His shoulders were stiff with anger that would weight his tongue and keep his face turned from me for hours. Anger also made him quicken his stride, gear after gear, until I could no longer keep up. I had forty-nine years on my legs and heart and lungs, while Jesse had only seventeen on his. My left foot ached from old bone breaks and my right knee creaked from recent surgery. Used to breathing among the low, muggy hills of Indiana, I was gasping up here in the alpine air, a mile and a half above sea level. Jesse would not stop, would not even slow down unless I asked; and I was in no mood to ask. So I slumped against a boulder beside the trail and let him rush on ahead.

This day, our first full one in Rocky Mountain National Park, had started out well. I woke at first light, soothed by the roar of a river foaming along one edge of the campground, and looked out from our tent to find half a dozen elk, all cows and calves, grazing so close by that I could see the gleam of their teeth. Just beyond the elk, a pair of ground squirrels loafed at the lip of their burrow, noses twitching. Beyond the squirrels, a ponderosa pine, backlit by sunrise, caught the wind in its ragged limbs. The sky was a blue slate marked only by the curving flight of swallows.

Up to that point, and for several hours more, the day was equally unblemished. Jesse slept on while I sipped coffee and studied maps and soaked in the early light. We made our plans over breakfast without squabbling: walk to Bridal Veil Falls in the morning, raft on the Cache la Poudre River in the afternoon, return to camp in the evening to get ready for backpacking up into Wild Basin the next day. Tomorrow we would be heavily laden, but today we carried only water and snacks, and I felt buoyant as we hiked along Cow Creek toward the waterfall. We talked easily the whole way, joking and teasing, more like good friends than like father and son. Yet even as we sat at the base of the falls, our shoulders touching, the mist of Bridal Veil cooling our skin, we remained father and son, locked in a struggle that I could only partly understand.

For the previous year or so, no matter how long our spells of serenity, Jesse and I had kept falling into quarrels, like victims of malaria breaking out in fever. We might be talking about soccer or supper, about the car keys or the news, and suddenly our voices would begin to clash like swords. I had proposed this trip to the mountains in hopes of discovering the source of that strife. Of course I knew that teenage sons and their fathers are expected to fight, yet I sensed there was a grievance between us that ran deeper than the usual vexations. Jesse was troubled by more than a desire to run his own life, and I was troubled by more than the pain of letting him go. I wished to track our anger to its lair, to find where it hid and fed and grew, and then, if I could not slay the demon, at least I could drag it into the light and call it by name.

The peace between us held until we turned back from the waterfall and began discussing where to camp the following night. Jesse wanted to push on up to Thunder Lake, near eleven thousand feet, and pitch our tent on snow. I wanted to stop a thousand feet lower and sleep on dry dirt.

"We're not equipped for snow," I told him.

"Sure we are. Why do you think I bought a new sleeping bag? Why did I call ahead to reserve snowshoes?"

I suggested that we could hike up from a lower campsite and snowshoe to his heart's content.

He loosed a snort of disgust. "I can't believe you're wimping out on me, Dad."

"I'm just being sensible."

"You're wimping out. I came here to see the backcountry, and all you want to do is poke around the foothills."

"This isn't wild enough for you?" I waved my arms at the view. "What do you need—avalanches and grizzlies?"

Just then, as we rounded a bend, an elderly couple came shuffling toward us, hunched over walking sticks, white hair jutting from beneath their straw hats. They were followed by three toddling children, each rigged out with tiny backpack and canteen. Jesse and I stood aside and let them pass, returning nods to their cheery hellos.

After they had trooped by, Jesse muttered, "We're in the wilds huh, Dad? That's why the trail's full of grandparents and kids." Then he quickened his pace until the damp blond curls that dangled below his billed cap were slapping against his neck.

"Is this how it's going to be?" I called after him. "You're going to spoil the trip because I won't agree to camp on snow?"

He turned and glared at me. "You're the one who's spoiling it, you and your hangups. You always ruin everything."

With that, he swung his face away and lengthened his stride and rushed on ahead. I watched his rigid shoulders and the bruise-colored patches on the back of his T-shirt until he disappeared beyond a rise. That was when I gave up on chasing him, slumped against a boulder and sucked at the thin air. Butterflies dallied around my boots and hawks kited on the breeze, but they might have been blips on a screen, and the whole panorama of snowy peaks and shimmering aspens and shining pines might have been cut from cardboard, for all the feeling they stirred in me.

The rocks that give these mountains their name are ancient, nearly a third as old as the earth, but the Rockies themselves are new, having been lifted up only six or seven million years ago, and they were utterly new to me, for I had never seen them before except from airplanes. I had been yearning toward them since I was Jesse's age, had been learning about their natural and human history, the surge of stone and gouge of glaciers, the wandering of hunters and wolves. Drawn to these mountains from the rumpled quilt of fields and forests in the hill country of the Ohio Valley, I was primed for splendor. And yet now that I was here I felt blinkered and numb.

What we call landscape is a stretch of earth overlaid with memory, expectation, and thought. Land is everything that is actually *there*, independent of us; landscape is what we allow in through the doors of perception. My own doors had slammed shut. My quarrel with Jesse changed nothing about the Rockies, but changed everything in my experience of the place. What had seemed glorious and vibrant when we set out that morning now seemed bleak and bare. It was as though anger had drilled a hole in the world and leached the color away.

I was still simmering when I caught up with Jesse at the trailhead, where he was leaning against our rented car, arms crossed over his chest, head sunk forward in a sullen pose I knew all too well, eyes hidden beneath the frayed bill of his cap. Having to wait for me to unlock the car had no doubt reminded him of another gripe: I carried the only set of keys. Because he was too young to be covered by the rental company's insurance, I would not let him drive. He had fumed about my decision, interpreting it as proof that I mistrusted him, still thought of him as a child. That earlier scuffle had petered out with him grumbling, "Stupid, stupid. I knew this would happen. Why did I come out here? Why?"

The arguments all ran together, playing over and over in my head as we jounced, too fast, along a rutted gravel road toward the highway. The tires whumped and the small engine whined up hills and down, but the silence inside the car was louder. We had two hours of driving to our rendezvous spot for the rafting trip, and I knew that Jesse could easily clamp his jaw shut for that long, and longer. I glanced over at him from time to time, looking for any sign of detente. His eyes were glass.

We drove. In the depths of Big Thompson Canyon, where the road swerved along a frothy river between sheer rockface and spindly guardrail, I could bear the silence no longer. "So what are my hang-ups?" I demanded. "How do I ruin everything?"

"You don't want to know," he said.

"I want to know. What is it about me that grates on you?"

I do not pretend to recall the exact words we hurled at one another after my challenge, but I remember the tone and thrust of them, and here is how they have stayed with me:

"You wouldn't understand," he said.

"Try me."

He cut a look at me, shrugged, then stared back through the windshield. "You're just so out of touch."

"With what?"

"With my whole world. You hate everything that's fun. You hate television and movies and video games. You hate my music."

"I like some of your music. I just don't like it loud."

"You hate advertising," he said quickly, rolling now. "You hate billboards and lotteries and developers and logging companies and big corporations. You hate snowmobiles and jet skis. You hate malls and fashions and cars."

"You're still on my case because I won't buy a Jeep?" I said, harking back to another old argument.

"Forget Jeeps. You look at any car and all you think is pollution, traffic, roadside crap. You say fast-food's poisoning our bodies and TV's poisoning our minds. You think the Internet is just another scam for selling stuff. You think business is a conspiracy to rape the earth."

"None of that bothers you?"

"Of course it does. But that's the *world*. That's where we've got to live. It's not going to go away just because you don't approve. What's the good of spitting on it?"

"I don't spit on it. I grieve over it."

He was still for a moment, then resumed quietly. "What's the good of grieving if you can't change anything?"

"Who says you can't change anything?"

"You do. Maybe not with your mouth, but with your eyes." Jesse rubbed his own eyes, and the words came out muffled through his cupped palms. "Your view of things is totally dark. It bums me out. You make me feel the planet's dying and people are to blame and nothing can be done about it. There's no room for hope. Maybe you can get by without hope, but I can't. I've got a lot of living still to do. I have to believe there's a way we can get out of this mess. Otherwise what's the point? Why study, why work— why do anything if it's all going to hell?"

That sounded unfair to me, a caricature of my views, and I thought of many sharp replies; yet there was too much truth and too much hurt in what he said for me to fire back an answer. Had I really deprived my son of hope? Was this the deeper grievance— that I had passed on to him, so young, my anguish over the world? Was this what lurked between us, driving us apart, the demon called despair?

"You're right," I finally told him. "Life's meaningless without hope. But I think you're wrong to say I've given up."

"It seems that way to me. As if you think we're doomed."

"No, buddy, I don't think we're doomed. It's just that nearly everything I care about is under assault."

"See, that's what I mean. You're so worried about the fate of the earth, you can't enjoy anything. We come to these mountains and you bring the shadows with you. You've got me seeing nothing but darkness."

Stunned by the force of his words, I could not speak. If my gloom cast a shadow over Creation for my son, then I had failed him. What remedy could there be for such a betrayal?

Through all the shouting and then talking and then the painful hush, our car hugged the swerving road, yet I cannot remember steering. I cannot remember seeing the stony canyon, the white mane of the Big Thompson whipping along beside us, the oncoming traffic. Somehow we survived our sashay with the river and cruised into a zone of burger joints and car-care emporiums and trinket shops. I realized how often, how relentlessly, I had groused about just this sort of "commercial dreck," and how futile my complaints must have seemed to Jesse.

He was caught between a chorus of voices telling him that the universe was made for us—that the earth is an inexhaustible warehouse, that consumption is the goal of life, that money is the road to delight—and the stubborn voice of his father saying none of this is so. If his father was right, then much of what humans babble every day—in ads and editorials, in sitcoms and song lyrics, in thrillers and market reports and teenage gab—is a monstrous lie. Far more likely that his father was wrong, deluded, perhaps even mad.

We observed an unofficial truce for the rest of the way to the gas station north of Fort Collins, where we met the rafting crew at noon. There had been record rains and snowfall in the Rockies for the previous three months, so every brook and river tumbling down from the mountains was frenzied and fast. When local people heard that we meant to raft the Cache la Poudre in this rough season they frowned and advised against it, recounting stories of broken legs, crushed skulls, deaths. Seeing that we were determined to go, they urged us to settle for the shorter trip that joined the river below the canyon, where the water spread out and calmed down. But Jesse had his heart set on taking the wildest ride available, so we had signed up for the twelve-mile trip through the boulder-strewn canyon.

I was relieved to see that the crowd of twenty or so waiting at the rendezvous point included scrawny kids and rotund parents. If the outfitters were willing to haul such passengers, how risky could the journey be? The sky-blue rafts, stacked on trailers behind yellow vans, looked indestructible. The guides seemed edgy, however, as they told us what to do if we were flung into the river, how to survive a tumble over rocks, how to get out from under a flipped raft, how to drag a flailing comrade back on board.

Jesse stood off by himself and listened to these dire instructions with a sober face. I could see him preparing, gaze focused inward, lips tight, the way he concentrated before taking his place in goal at a soccer game.

When the time came for us to board the vans, he and I turned out to be the only customers for the canyon run; all the others, the reedy kids and puffing parents, were going on the tamer trip. Our raft would be rolled out by three sinewy young men, students at Colorado State who were being paid to risk their necks: a guide with a year's experience and two trainees.

The water in Poudre Canyon looked murderous, all spume and standing waves and suckholes and rips. Every cascade, every low bridge, every jumble of boulders reminded the guides of some disaster, which they rehearsed with gusto. It was part of their job to crank up the thrill, I knew that, but I also knew from talking with friends that most of the tales were true.

At the launching spot, Jesse and I wriggled into our black wetsuits, cinched tight the orange flotation vests, buckled on white helmets. The sight of my son in that armor sent a blade of anxiety through me again. What if he got hurt? Lord God, what if he were killed?

"Hey, Dad," Jesse called, hoisting a paddle in his fist, "you remember how to use one of these?"

"Seems like I remember teaching *you*," I called back.

He flashed me a grin, the first sign of communication since we had sat with shoulders touching in the mist of Bridal Veil Falls. That one look restored me to my senses, and I felt suddenly the dazzle of sunlight, heard the river's rumble and the fluting of birds, smelled pine sap and wet stone.

One of the trainees, a lithe wisecracker named Harry, would guide our run. "If it gets quiet in back," he announced, "that means I've fallen in and somebody else better take over."

We clambered into the raft—Jesse and I up front, the veteran guide and the other trainee in the middle, Harry in the stern. Each of us hooked one foot under a loop sewn into the rubbery floor, jammed the other foot under a thwart. Before we hit the first rapids, Harry made us practice synchronizing our strokes as he hollered, "Back paddle! Forward paddle! Stop! Left turn! Right turn!" The only other command, he explained, was "Jump!" Hearing that, the paddlers on the side away from some looming boulder or snag were to heave themselves *toward* the obstruction, in order to keep the raft from flipping.

"I know it sounds crazy," said Harry. "But it works. And remember: from now on, if you hear fear in my voice, it's real."

Fear was all I felt over the next few minutes, a bit for myself and a lot for Jesse, as we struck white water and the raft began to buck. Waves slammed against the bow, spray flew, stone whizzed by. A bridge swelled ahead of us, water boiling under the low arches, and Harry shouted, "Duck!" then steered us between the lethal pilings and out the other side into more rapids, where he yelled, "Left turn! Dig hard! Harder!"

He kept barking orders, and soon I was too busy paddling to feel anything except my own muscles pulling against the great writhing muscle of the river. I breathed in as much water as air. The raft spun and dipped and leapt with ungainly grace, sliding through narrow flumes, gliding over rocks, kissing cliffs and bouncing away, yielding to the grip of the currents and springing free. Gradually I sank into my body.

The land blurred past. Sandstone bluffs rose steeply along one shore, then the other, then both—hundreds of feet of rock pinching the sky high above into a ribbon of blue. Here and there a terrace opened, revealing a scatter of junipers and scrub cedars, yet before I could spy what else might be growing there, it jerked away out of sight. I could tell only that this was dry country, harsh and spare, with dirt the color of scrap iron and gouged by erosion. Every time I tried to fix on a detail, on bird or flower or stone, a shout from Harry yanked me back to the swing of the paddle.

The point of our bucking ride, I realized, was not to see the canyon but to survive it. The river was our bronco, our bull, and the land through which it flowed was no more present to us than the rodeo's dusty arena to a whirling cowboy. Haste hid the country, dissolved the landscape, as surely as anger or despair ever did.

"Forward paddle!" Harry shouted. "Give me all you've got! We're coming to the Widow-Maker! Let's hope we come out alive!"

The flooded Poudre, surging through its crooked canyon, was a string of emergencies, each one christened with an ominous name. In a lull between rapids, I glanced over at Jesse, and he was beaming. His helmet seemed to strain from the expansive pressure of his smile. I laughed aloud to see him. When he was little I could summon that look of unmixed delight into his face merely by coming home, opening my arms, and calling, "Where's my boy?" In his teenage years, the look had become rare, and it hardly ever had anything to do with me.

"Jump!" Harry shouted.

Before I could react, Jesse lunged at me and landed heavily and the raft bulged over a boulder, nearly tipping, then righted itself and plunged on downstream.

"Good job!" Harry crowed. "That was a close one."

Jesse scrambled back to his post. "You okay?" he asked.

"Sure," I answered. "How about you?"

"Great," he said. "Fantastic."

For the remaining two hours of our romp down the Poudre I kept stealing glances at Jesse, who paddled as though his life truly depended on how hard he pulled. His face shone with joy, and my own joy was kindled from seeing it.

This is an old habit of mine, the watching and weighing of my son's experience. Since his birth I have enveloped him in a cloud of thought. How's he doing? I wonder. Is he hungry? Hurting? Tired? Is he grumpy or glad? Like so many other exchanges between parent and child, this concern flows mainly one way; Jesse does not surround me with thought. On the contrary, with each passing year he pays less and less attention to me, except when he needs something, and then he bristles at being reminded of his dependence. That's natural, mostly, although teenage scorn for parents also gets a boost from popular culture. My own father had to die before I thought seriously about what he might have needed or wanted or suffered. If Jesse has children of his own one day, no doubt he will brood on them as I have brooded on him for these seventeen years. Meanwhile, his growing up requires him to break free of my concern. I accept that, yet I cannot turn off my fathering mind.

Before leaving for Colorado, I had imagined that he would be able to meet the Rockies with clear eyes, with the freshness of his green age. So long as he was in my company, however, he would see the world through the weather of my moods. And if despair had so darkened my vision that I was casting a shadow over Jesse's world, even here among these magnificent mountains and tumultuous rivers, then I would have to change. I would have to learn to see differently. Since I could not forget the wounds to people and planet, could not unlearn the dismal numbers—the tallies of pollution and population and poverty that foretold catastrophe—I would have to look harder for antidotes, for medicines, for sources of hope.

Tired and throbbing from the river trip, we scarcely spoke during the long drive back to our campground in the national park. This time, though, the silence felt easy, like a fullness rather than a void.

In that tranquility I recalled our morning's hike to Bridal Veil Falls before the first quarrel of the day. No matter how briskly I walked, Jesse kept pulling ahead. He seemed to be in a race, eyes focused far up the trail, as though testing himself against the rugged terrain. I had come to this high country for a holiday from rushing. A refugee from the tyranny of deadlines and destinations, I wished to linger, squatting over the least flower or fern, reading the braille of bark with my fingers, catching the notes of water and birds and wind. But Jesse was just as intent on covering ground. Although we covered the same ground, most of the time we experienced quite different landscapes, his charged with trials of endurance, mine with trials of perception. Then every once in a while the land brought us together—in the mist of the falls, on the back of the river—and it was as if, for a moment, the same music played in both of us.

Without any quarrel to distract me, I watched the road faithfully as we wound our way up through Big Thompson Canyon. We entered the park at dusk. A rosy light glinted on the frozen peaks of the Front Range.

I was driving slowly, on the lookout for wildlife, when a coyote loped onto the road ahead of us, paused halfway across, then stared back in the direction from which it had come. As we rolled to a stop, a female elk came charging after, head lowered and teeth bared. The coyote bounded away, scooted up a bank on the far side of the road, then paused to peer back over its bony shoulder. Again the elk charged; again the coyote pranced away, halted, stared. Jesse and I watched this ballet of taunting and chasing, taunting and chasing, until the pair vanished over a ridge.

"What was that all about?" he asked when we drove on.

"She was protecting a calf, I expect."

"You mean a coyote can eat an elk?"

"The newborns they can."

When I shut off the engine at the campground and we climbed out of the car, it was as though we had stepped back into the raft, for the sound of rushing water swept over us. The sound lured us downhill to the bank of a stream, and we sat there soaking in the watery music until our bellies growled. We made supper while the full moon chased Jupiter and Mars up the arc of the sky. The flame on our stove flounced in a northerly breeze, promising cool weather for tomorrow's hike into Wild Basin.

We left the flap of our tent open so we could lie on our backs and watch the stars burn fiercely in the mountain air. Our heads were so close together that I could hear Jesse's breath, even above the shoosh of the river, and I could tell he was nowhere near sleep.

"I feel like I'm still on the water," he said after a spell, "and the raft's bobbing under me and the waves are crashing all around."

"I feel it too."

"That's one of the things I wanted to be sure and do before things fall apart."

I rolled onto my side and propped my head on an elbow and looked at his moonlit profile. "Things don't *have* to fall apart, buddy."

"Maybe not." He blinked, and the spark in his eyes went out and relit. "I just get scared."

"So do I. But the earth's a tough old bird. And we should be smart enough to figure out how to live here."

"Let's hope." There was the scritch of a zipper and a thrashing of legs, and Jesse sprawled on top of his new sleeping bag, which was too warm for this fifty-degree night. "I guess things could be scarier," he said. "Imagine being an elk, never knowing what's sneaking up on you."

"Or a coyote," I said, "never knowing where you'll find your next meal."

A great horned owl called. Another answered, setting up a duet across our valley. We listened until they quit.

"You know," said Jesse. "I've been thinking. Maybe we don't need to sleep on snow. Maybe we can pitch camp in the morning at North St. Vrain, where there ought to be some bare ground, then we can snowshoe up to Thunder Lake in the afternoon."

"You wouldn't be disappointed if we did that? Wouldn't feel we'd wimped out?"

"Naw," he said. "That's cool."

"Then that's the plan, man."

The stars burned on. The moon climbed. Just when I thought he was asleep, Jesse murmured, "How's that knee?"

"Holding up so far," I told him, surprised by the question, and only then did I notice the aching in my knee and foot.

"Glad to hear it. I don't want to be lugging you out of the mountains."

When he was still young enough to ride in a backpack I had lugged him to the tops of mountains and through dripping woods and along the slate beds of creeks and past glittering windows on city streets, while he burbled and sang over my shoulder; but I knew better than to remind him of that now in his muscular youth. I lay quietly, following the twin currents of the river and my son's breath. Here were two reasons for rejoicing, two sources of hope. For Jesse's sake, and for mine, I would get up the next morning and hunt for more.

Gardening with the Raucous Fairy

My attempt at a tranquil moment weeding in the yard before bed seemed a twisted joke when my five- and seven-year-old sons went back to the house, found the pointy adult kitchen shears, and after a few moments of harmlessly cutting and eating chives, began jabbing them at each other.

"Not to hurt each other," Mercury, the oldest, protested indignantly as I grabbed the scissors.

Solly, the two-year-old who had, thankfully, not even had a pair of scissors, dissolved into a tantrum. "I want scissors! I want scissors! I want scissors!"

"I have no use for you." The oldest stalked off. "I don't like you."

I clenched my teeth. It had been a long day. That morning the boys had woken just as I was slipping out of bed for a few moments of quiet. They'd mounded like puppies in my bed, wriggling and wrestling, at first joyful with the fight, but within moments Nashua's elbow jabbed hard against Solly's face and Solly bit him. After I calmed them and put Solly in time-out, they wanted escorts to the bathroom, glasses of water, and breakfast.

Now it was evening. The day had been irritatingly hot as I poured drinks and pulled fighting boys apart again and again, and I craved those few moments of cool quiet time I'd missed that morning. I would, I simply *would*, have ten minutes without

33

conflict, in peace, weeding my corn which was, at this point, no longer visible.

I put the scissors up, way up, and grabbed Mercury and Nashua by the arms and yanked them over to the corn bed. "We are gardening," I said, and added, "together, as a family," not because I wanted to but because I clearly couldn't let them out of my sight.

"How *boring*," said Mercury, who had reached an age when he could tell the difference between a vegetable and a weed and had some weeding experience.

"Oh *well*," I said. And there must have been something very special about the way I said it, maybe the angry hissing sound, because he sat down and began tugging out the leafy, green, foot-tall pig weed.

"Nashua and Solly, take these weeds to the goats." I indicated a pile I had already pulled. They also decided to take me seriously. They picked up a few weeds and ran the short distance to the goat pen.

The evening was a perfect late-June eastern Washington evening. The earth breathed again after the hot day. Coolness pooled near the ground and blew gently on my skin. The earth oozed a rich, deep, primal smell that all day had been masked by the brittle dustiness of heat. I breathed deeply. Pine forests cast long shadows across the fields. Minutes stretched. When I was a child I used to walk in the forest on such evenings, nearly past my bedtime, to see the flowers and look for fairies. And while I'm not particularly inclined to believe in fairies anymore, something magical happened this June night.

Mercury began to concentrate on freeing our little corn, squash, and bean plants from the thick green mass that now completely covered the garden. He sought the tiny bean plants under the lushness and untangled the spindly squash vines that had curled themselves around the monstrous pig weed.

We could barely keep Nashua supplied with weeds for the goats, and he was impatient if we did not have a pile big enough to warrant a trip.

"I am feeding the goats a good dinner," he informed us. "I tell them, 'Here is cream pie.'"

"We are rescuing the good plants from the bad plants," Mercury told me, raising his arm above the weeds. "We are an airplane heading for the attack." His arm dove into the weeds.

Nashua quickly appreciated the new scenario.

"The goats are gobbling up the bad plants," he told us on his next return.

"The bad plant are bombs," Mercury said. "We are transporting them to the giant pen where giants without arms destroy them."

I kept weeding, enjoying the air on my skin, happy the boys were engaged. Then I noticed that yanking the monstrous plants *did* seem like destroying an enemy. Freeing the tiny plants, yellowed and stunted from their life below the weeds, *did* feel like liberating them from a dark enemy prison.

"We welcome you to the world of sun and water," I said to a tiny bean plant I'd found hunkered against the dirt.

The boys embraced my addition to their game and began welcoming their plants to freedom. Suddenly we were all involved in a full-fledged war. Our airplanes dove and attacked in mid-air. They dropped bombs. Ground forces drove back the approaching cavalry. These armies hacked giant warriors and felled mighty fortresses. We all cheered on the goats, who ripped voraciously into the piles of weeds, doing the final destruction.

We weeded faster and faster, anxious for an ultimate victory. Row after row of plants sprang free from the oppression of dark, viciousness, and evil.

"This is the funnest farming activity ever," Nashua said.

"I never want to go in," Mercury told me.

The evening darkened, and I suspected it was past nine. The youngest began to get fussy. I broke the news to the boys that it really was bedtime.

They were so happy they did not care. Tomorrow, they said, we can save the good guys from the bad guys again. I reluctantly began to get ready to go in too. This half hour had been the most relaxed, happy, family time of the day, even though it was nothing like my image of tranquil garden time. If there was a fairy responsible here, it was not one of those tiny ballerina-like fairies with wings I always sought under flowers. They never play war games. No, our fairy was a big muscular fairy with a twisted grin who laughed a raucous laugh and bathed regularly in squirts of testosterone. But he still knew about peace, so I shrugged, threw my visions to the night air, and said "thank you" for what was.

Jack Nisbet

Deadfall

The day our family moved to a new neighborhood in Spokane, my daughter Emily and I decided to descend from the lip of the plateau where the house was located to a creek several hundred feet below. We switchbacked across a dry open slope for twenty minutes or so and were just entering some thicker woods when we passed a medium-sized ponderosa pine snag that leaned over the trail. The snag looked to be on its last legs, with red-orange bark scaling away, and it had already shed several large upper branches. A fire scar at the base of the trunk looked like an old but still debilitating wound. Certain that the pine was about to fall, Emily refused to walk under it. We stepped off the trail and stretched our hands along the dead wood, pushing together to test its strength. When the snag bounced rhythmically back, I convinced her there was nothing to do but keep walking.

Emily made a show of hesitating, then dashed beneath the snag in a low duckwalk of a crouch. Just clear of its shadow she crouched again, this time to pick up a piece of paper from the ground. It was a page torn from a paperback book, one corner singed black and still smelling of smoke. A freshening breeze rustled several more pages that upon inspection proved to be fragments of a flighty romance novel. Emily lingered in the shadow of the snag so she could digest them—she was eleven and had always liked to read.

That sidehill led to miles of trails that crisscrossed eroding bluffs on their way down to the winding creek, and over the course of the next seven years we explored them a couple of times a week. Although the slopes offered their fair share of natural wonders and seasonal change, we soon found ourselves going out by force of habit, just to get the dog some air and walk off the day's small events. Because we were father and daughter, often we began our strolls complaining or walking apart; on more than a few occasions we spit angry words while the crossbills kipped above us. The bluffs held their less pleasant aspects as well, from eroding cutoff trails to the way noxious weeds kept encroaching on the native bunchgrass and wildflowers. But such distractions were dwarfed by the fact that the regular walks allowed us, with a continuity enforced by familiar landmarks, to carry on an endless conversation about what was going on outside and inside our respective heads.

During that lucky span, the leaning ponderosa snag slowly proceeded on its road to ruin, shedding more bark and branches. Wind and snow polished the spiral growth of the naked trunk to a pearly gray. Around the fire scar, contorted sapwood slowly unpeeled from the heart. Every time we passed the tree Emily would duck hurriedly underneath exactly as she had on our first encounter, stopping our flow of talk like a prayer bell interrupting steady meditation. But when the time came for Emily to leave home entirely, the snag had still not toppled.

Until I started to bug him about it, the only story my dad ever told about his father, Edwin, involved a huge oak tree that dominated the edge of one of the family fields. It was a very brief tale that began on a hot summer afternoon in South Carolina. Edwin's cows gathered in a clump under the protection of this red oak's crown, pawing at the red clay around its roots as above them black anvil clouds banged up a thunderstorm. My grandfather was thinking that if the skies finally opened he would need to seek shelter there himself, when suddenly a tremendous crack of lightning struck every one of those cows dead at the foot of the ruling oak. That was the end of the story, and no matter how many times I made my dad tell it, Edwin never reappeared to assess the damage. What does a Depression-era cotton farmer do with thirty dead cows?

Although Edwin died some years before I was born, his farm stayed in the family, and I came to associate him with a red oak snag that stood behind an old tool shed on the home place. That tree, which may well have been killed by a lightning strike, had hardened into a solid block six or eight feet around, and my uncle used to delight in sending my cousins and me out to chop it into firewood. In a contest that lasted for years, all of our most diligent ax blows bounced off the oak with tuneless clunks. It was as if Edwin himself were wrapped up in the iron wood, a trunk full of undiscovered treasure whose lock we couldn't quite crack.

Just as I never met my grandfather Edwin, Emily never met my mother, Kay. But perhaps because my dad's single take on the subject of his father had left me so unsatisfied, I thought I had a whole lot better stories to tell about Kay—she seemed to me full of contradictions and rough edges, with the kind of odd obsessions that struck the memory hard. The way I remembered it, my mother had carefully taught her children to capture June bugs in our hands so we could admire their shiny backs. She helped us transform shoe boxes into square worlds full of dirt and twigs for stag beetles to explore. It was Kay who supplied the Mason jars and cheesecloth for endless summer nights of firefly chasing, and doped those same Mason jars with spot remover that anesthetized the walking sticks we brought back from the woods. She liked to pin the results of our insect hunts in cardboard cases, hanging with us as we tried to keep the bodies in one piece and the bright colors from fading. We'd hold them up together and lament that they never quite looked alive.

Kay's pointed enthusiasm did not necessarily transfer to the pine trees down the bluff, however, and when an array of long-horned bark beetles failed to capture Emily's interest, I wondered how much of it might have been a product of my imagination. It soon dawned on me that because Kay had passed away so early, there were many parts of her I was still trying to sort out for myself, and perhaps I should consider a bit more carefully which stories about her spilled out. Then I began to wonder what else my dad might have been thinking about when he made that bolt of lightning strike the oak tree so close to Edwin.

On succeeding trips down the bluff, I decided not to tell Emily that the way the ponderosa snag arched painfully over the trail reminded me of Kay's brief experiments in bonsai, and how I had been perplexed by her awkward attempts to contort a mugo pine with loops of cotton twine. When in early May the mock orange bloomed in profusion along the hillside, I kept it to myself how their scent brought back my mother's prized gardenia bush. It had been my job to pour the iced tea leaves out on it every evening after supper, but Kay was the one who clipped a single waxy white blossom in the morning to float, fragrant, in her special pewter bowl.

While I kept such intimate thoughts unspoken for a while, Emily had no trouble releasing hers. Often they involved her latest reading explorations, such as explaining the unspoken laws of the Green and Blue Fairy books. For months she delved into wild overlapping Northern myths that ranged from Scotland to Siberia, which were always great fun to retell. As she added to the canon step by step along the trail, I realized that this was not the first time such legends had been offered to me — Kay had also been a fan of selkies, and Loki, and Baba Yaga. When Emily progressed to the gender-bending plot lines of a female Japanese comic artist, I responded with a curious but befuddled attraction, soaking up the tone of their exotic magic without understanding it at all. In my early teens those same qualities had drawn me to a collection of J.D. Salinger stories that I had seen my mother reading, but I stopped short of trying to explain the connection to Emily.

Curling among such manga, mythology, and popular fiction came C.S. Lewis, whose *Chronicles of Narnia* continually cropped up in Emily's conversation. She had read them first before we ever hit the bluffs but took them up again whenever she felt the need, I think because of the way they seemed to feed her spiritual desires. Kay had read the successive volumes of the *Chronicles* to my younger sisters, but I refused to go anywhere near Narnia until Emily sold me on the elegance of its history. It was under her spell that I finally came alive when the wardrobe opened up, and when I felt the terrible blow of the final train crash that seemed to snuff things out in a way that let them start all over again. It was only after dozens of such lessons that I recalled the way Kay had clung to another C.S. Lewis volume called *A Grief Observed*. That book had been popular at the same time as Salinger's *Franny and Zooey* sagas but had remained beneath her bedside lamp for a much longer run.

I only knew this because of one particular morning when I needed my mother to solve some problem that seemed a little desperate at the time. She failed to answer any of my repeated calls, so I searched house and yard thoroughly, moving faster and faster until I finally burst into my parents' bedroom. There, to my utter shock, I discovered Kay kneeling silently by her bed, leaning forward like a supplicant. Those same bony fingers that had recently pried a Polyphemus moth from a collecting jar were now twisted up in prayer, all ligaments and knuckles and discomfort. When she looked up at me she did not utter a single word. I could only stare at her bedside table and the vaguely purple jacket of *A Grief Observed* as I backed carefully away from her sanctuary.

Strolling through the pine woods, I decided to drip this information slowly to Emily—not certain that such twisted emotions were exactly the qualities it was my duty to pass on, yet knowing at the same time that it was entirely her gift to me. By following the course of her own intense and random interests, Emily had somehow found ways of connecting with an interior Kay whom I had barely touched. Without my daughter, I never would have felt the full power of my mother's prayer.

I had barely managed a stuttered beginning to that acciden-
tal bedroom interruption before we approached the leaning snag.
Emily's mind appeared to be somewhere else entirely, but as
she crouched beneath the pine she reached up and touched its
twisted trunk with both her hands. She allowed her palms to rest
there for a moment, as if offering a prayer of her own. Then she
stood upright on the path and resumed her long strides up the
hill.

Martha Beck

Expecting Adam

Every December my friend Annette, who in other respects is a very nice person, spends an inordinate amount of time and money obtaining the most obnoxious toy gun on the market for Adam's Christmas present. I don't give my children guns as toys, but as Adam's honorary auntie, Annette feels that it is her right and responsibility to indulge the kid's most violent, macho, antisocial tendencies.

Adam loves her very much.

Annette's first criterion, when purchasing the Christmas gun, is wattage. She looks for a product that makes enough noise to disrupt the breeding process for every bird within a mile radius of our house. Flashing lights rank a close second. Annette prefers guns that flash several colors, all bright enough to stun the average person's retina, so that for a couple of minutes after Adam fires the gun at you, you walk blindly into walls and pillars and closed glass doors. It is also very important to have an innovative design, with various exotic flanges meant to suggest deadliness of interplanetary proportions.

It goes without saying that guns of this magnitude require dozens of large batteries. Annette never forgets this; she always buys an ample supply of them, wrapping them in a separate package, which she tapes to the actual gun. I'm telling you, the woman has absolutely no mercy.

The first Christmas after Annette and I got to know each other, my children arose at a predictably ungodly hour and descended on their gifts like locusts on an alfalfa field. Along with most other American parents, John and I had spent a good part of the previous month tracking down the items our children had requested in their letters to Santa. Katie had asked for a set of birdcalls she'd seen in an FAO Schwarz catalog. Five-year-old Lizzie wanted one of those dolls they advertise on Saturday morning cartoons, the ones that have repulsively cute names and have been engineered to mimic the least pleasant behaviors of real human babies. I think that year Lizzie's doll had an anxiety-related bed-wetting disorder or something. Adam wanted a whole brigade of toys with names like Cretin Slime Monsters.

In the proud tradition of delayed gratification John inherited from a long line of Becks, the children opened their presents one by one. Katie went first. The FAO Schwarz birdcall set had turned out to cost several hundred dollars, so John and I had purchased what we thought was a reasonable facsimile. It didn't cover quite as broad an ornithological spectrum as the pricier set, but it could produce a great duck sound, a good owl, and several very convincing songbirds. When she saw it, Katie's face fell. It is an awful thing to see your kid's face fall on Christmas morning.

"Don't you like it?" I asked anxiously.

"No, no, it's okay. I like it." Katie smiled a stalwart smile, but her lower lip trembled ever so slightly. I began to feel that perhaps we should have taken out a second mortgage to pay for the FAO Schwarz birdcall set.

Lizzie went next. She tore the gift wrapping off the bed-wetting doll, and then she, too, developed the troubled look around the eyes.

"What's the matter?" I asked.

"Well," said Lizzie, with her high voice and precocious vocabulary, "it's not exactly what I asked for."

John, who had fought his way through about seventeen toy stores looking for that particular doll, burst out, "I thought you *wanted* Tiny Whiny Princess Wee-Wee!"

"I did," said Lizzie, "but I wanted the one with the *pink* jewels, and this one only has the *purple* jewels."

Within minutes, both the girls had reconciled themselves to their gifts. Like their pioneer ancestors, many of whom had died crossing the Great Plains on foot in the dead of winter, dragging their possessions behind them in handcarts, my daughters were able to steel themselves to the brutal realities of an imperfect world. This was good, because I had been on the verge of sending them both to military school.

Now it was Adam's turn. He fished around under the Christmas tree until he found a package with his name on it. It was from Annette. He tore the paper off, holding his breath, and found— batteries. An eight pack of double D's, still encased in plastic.

"Oh, honey," I said, "that's not the real present. The real present is—"

But Adam didn't hear me. He was staring at those batteries as if they were so magnificent he couldn't quite take them in. His mouth fell open in astonished ecstasy as he held the batteries up to the light.

"Oh, wow!" he said. "*Oh, wow!* Mom, look! *Batteries!*" (It actually sounded more like "*Mom, ook! Aggabies!*" but the message was clear.)

Before we could divert his attention to any other gift, Adam leapt to his feet and began running around the house, locating every appliance, tool, and toy that ran on batteries. The whole time, he babbled excitedly about all the things he could do with this fabulous, fabulous gift. As we watched, it began to occur to all of us "normal" people in the family that batteries really were a pretty darn good Christmas present. They didn't look like much, on the face of it, but think what they could *do*! Put them in place, and inanimate objects suddenly came to life, moving, talking, singing, lighting up the room. Something about Adam always manages to see straight past the outward ordinariness of a thing to any magic it may hold inside. We wouldn't even have bothered to let him open the gun, except we were afraid Annette would buy him a neutron bomb for his birthday if we didn't.

I bring this up because, looking back on the journal I kept while I was expecting Adam, I find that before he was even born, I was already comparing him to a disappointing holiday gift. I must mention that this journal was not meant to be read by others. It was the secret place where I poured out my most distasteful and shocking emotions, to keep myself from going insane during the endless, frightening months between his diagnosis and his birth.

"Last week," I wrote one January afternoon, "a homeless man I passed in Harvard Square took one look at my belly and said, 'Congratulations, Mamma!' I've almost forgotten what it was like to have people react that way. Nobody does, since we found out about the Down syndrome. The baby has become unmentionable, like a gift everyone knows is inferior and broken, before it's even unwrapped."

This comment was largely true, although perhaps a bit too absolute. Not "everyone" stopped treating me like a pregnant woman and began acting as if I'd contracted a terminal illness. But precious few of the exceptions came from within the Harvard community, the community that had been my reference group, my "ideal" culture, since I was seventeen years old. No one at Harvard seemed able to tolerate the thought of Santa's leaving the wrong kind of baby under the tree. It was very clear what kind of children most Harvard types would have asked for in their letters to Santa. I realized this not much more than an hour after I learned about Adam's Down syndrome.

I left the apartment soon after John came home. In our marriage, the unspoken rule had always been that when one of us was upset, the other would compensate by being strong and encouraging. We'd switch roles after the upset person began to feel a little better. It reminded me of mountaineering teams whose members take turns scaling unconquered territory, planting ropes on a vertical rock face and then helping their partners up a few feet. The day we found out about Adam strained this system to its breaking point. I was far too devastated to comfort John. Perhaps if he'd been any less tired or jet-lagged or worried about school, he could have soldiered through and comforted me. But he was already carrying a heavy burden, and the news that one's unborn son is going to be mentally retarded isn't merely a straw to break the camel's back. It's more like a sack of headstones.

It's painful to remember the way John's face looked when I told him; so painful that I can barely summon the memory. He went very, very pale. Then he came slowly over, as though he were sleepwalking, and put his arms around me. He was as cold as a statue.

"You're going to keep him, aren't you?" he said.

I nodded slowly, my face against his chest.

"So that's why," said John. "So that's why."

I looked up at him. "What do you mean?"

He was staring over my head at the window. The light that came from it was dim and gray.

"In the restaurant, that day," he said. "The day you got the tests done. You remember?"

I nodded again.

"We were sitting there, and you were talking about abortion, and then…" John's voice trailed off and he shook his head. "It was probably just my imagination. But it was so—so *strong*."

I felt a prickle of electricity go up my spine. I pulled back my head and looked up into his haggard, beloved face. "What was so strong?"

He closed his eyes and swallowed. Then he said, very reluctantly, "I heard this…voice."

I said nothing. I had known what he was going to tell me before he said it.

John continued even more slowly. "It said something."

I knew exactly what he was feeling, exactly why it seemed physically painful for him to tell me. He was fighting through the same walls of disbelief, the same fear of ridicule, the same shame I felt when I thought of talking to anyone about the inexplicable things that had happened to me. He didn't know about the decision I had made—to believe anything, everything, until it was proven false—and I was too stunned to explain.

I just asked, "What did it say?"

John shook his head, as though to apologize for what he was about to tell me. "It said, '*John, keep the baby.*'" John looked down at me, and his face suddenly looked concerned. "I mean, I know it isn't my decision, it's *your* decision, but—"

I set one finger on his lips. "It's okay," I said, although of course nothing was okay.

"The thing is," said John, "it wasn't like an order. It felt more like someone was giving me advice, someone who knew more than I did." He bit his lip hard, and I could see that the memory made him want to cry. "It sounded very kind," he concluded.

"I know," I said.

"Do you think I'm crazy?" John sounded like a little boy.

I shook my head. "Look what I'm doing," I said. I put a hand on my swollen midsection. "Do you think *I'm* crazy?"

He shook his head but said nothing. We were both too overwhelmed to talk anymore. I didn't know how to begin telling John about the Bunraku puppeteers, about the strange things I had experienced during the last five months. I was somewhat surprised and slightly comforted to know that John, too, had heard one of the voices, and I was immensely relieved that the experience seemed to have discouraged him from pressuring me to abort the baby. But what might have intrigued and excited me in different circumstances barely seemed worth thinking about now that I was trying to adjust to being the mother of a retarded child.

John and I stood there in silence for several minutes, until it was clear that neither one of us was prepared to be the strong one, to take the lead on this particular mountaineering expedition. We had reached a spot beyond our ability to cope as a team. So without another word, we disengaged, and each of us reverted to the behaviors we had used to cope with disturbing information for most of our lives.

For John, this meant a ferocious concentration on work. He went into a frenzy of activity, typing up notes for his dissertation, giving Katie her dinner, making phone calls to Singapore, doing the laundry. The movement of his mind and muscles, the simplicity and solidity of work, seemed to allow him to shut down his awareness of what was happening to his personal life. He was a Harvard kind of guy.

To me, John's behavior was incomprehensible. I couldn't focus on anything but my fear and grief. My way of coping with this situation—with any situation—was to learn everything I could about it, to follow my credo that knowledge is power. Knowledge had helped me dull the pain and fear of being different ever since I had learned how to talk. And so, before I even stopped at Judy Trenton's office on that day she called with the "not so good news," I made for the bookstore section of the Harvard Coop to look for information about raising a child with Down syndrome.

The Coop is Harvard's official bookstore, the one that stocks all the textbooks and required readings for classes. It sells everything from Harvard insignia T-shirts to snack foods, and it has one of the largest and best-equipped book sections of any college store in the country. I had never spent much time browsing the "parenting" section. Before Katie was born, I had a hard time believing that an actual baby was going to come out of me, let alone survive the event. After her birth, I was busy forcing myself through thousands of pages of required sociological theory—this at a time when I was too tired to really focus on anything longer than a haiku. I never got around to reading much about how to raise children, not even an article in *Woman's Day*. I decided that feeling guilty about *not* reading such things would have to be good enough.

At least I knew which section of the Coop contained books on parenting. I lugged my abdomen toward Harvard Square, keeping my eyes fixed on the cobblestones directly in front of me. This was how I kept myself from coming apart. I had never meditated before, but over the next few months I would figure out how to do it without any instruction at all. I learned to wash my mind blank and stare at some object, real or imagined, until I felt as though I were floating in a state of being that was nearly, but not precisely, alive. I devised mantras, phrases I repeated over and over to help me stop thinking. I remember vividly the mantra that got me from my apartment to the Coop that afternoon. As I walked along the slushy sidewalks under a freezing rain, I murmured over and over, "Why not me? Why not me? Why not me?"

I can honestly say I never did ask the opposite question. The answer seemed obvious. I have been the beneficiary of so much improbable good fortune in my life that it's only logical I'd have some bad luck as well. What I did ask myself that day, what I continue to ask myself as I watch Adam go out into a frightening world in all his gentleness, sweetness, and hope, is, "Why him? Why him? Why him?" The hardest lesson I have ever had to learn is that I will never know the meaning of my children's pain, and that I have neither the capacity nor the right to take it away from them.

It was the thought of Adam's pain that finally broke through my numbness and let the full weight of my emotion bear down on me. Even though I loved my unborn baby with unreasoning intensity, I was terribly afraid for him. I was also terribly afraid of him. The bulge of my torso now seemed freakish, monstrous, grotesque. The baby inside it was broken. He was substandard. He was not what I had wanted.

Once I got to the Coop and made my way to the parenting section, I found a lot of examples of what I *had* wanted laid out in front of me. Four or five long bookshelves were occupied by instructional variations on a single subject: how to turn a human infant into a genius in the shortest time possible. The object, apparently, was to have every child—no, I'm sorry, make that "*your* child"—contributing important innovations to science and letters before it achieved bowel control. There were books recommending different shapes to hang from mobiles, thus stimulating your infant's intellectual development. There were sets of flash cards designed to help your tiny scholar's mind associate phonetic symbols with the appropriate sounds. Others promoted development across the whole behavioral spectrum, teaching everything from ethics, to "killer competitiveness." I have seen many of these same books in other bookstores at other times, but only the Harvard Coop had all of them: *Teach Your Baby to Read; Born to Win; Pre-Law for Preschoolers; Toddling Through the Calculus.*

Staring at these titles through tear-glazed eyes, I felt like a kid holding a lump of coal, watching everyone else open gorgeous, desirable Tiny Whiny Princess Wee-Wees with the pink *and* purple jewels. For the first time in my life, I began to question why there should be so much material to help parents enhance their children's "excellence." Slowly, slowly, standing in the Coop, I realized that I was not looking for information to transform my child into a prize every parent would envy. I needed to transform myself into a parent who could accept her child, no matter what. There were no books for that in the parenting section of the Harvard Coop.

I left the parenting section without buying anything and proceeded up the escalator to the textbook section. There, after a half hour's search through the textbooks for abnormal psychology classes, I found a small book on how to train and teach the mentally retarded. The book was a mustard-yellow paperback with a photograph of two children on the cover. They both had Down syndrome. The picture was grainy and out of focus; the two children, lumpish and awkward-looking, stared dully at the camera through small, misshapen eyes. I cannot tell you how much it hurt me to look at that picture. It was like getting my heart caught in a mill saw.

I turned the book facedown and carried it to the cash register, focusing on the grimy linoleum floor tiles to keep my mind in suspended animation. Why not me? Why not me? Why not me? The woman at the cash register flipped the book over, and I saw the picture again. I almost ran for the door. I forced myself to look at the book's cover again as I handed over my money. Those two children in the picture were everything I had ever learned to avoid. Beneath a thin facade of polite pity, I found in myself a roiling sea of fear and loathing. The words that sprang to my mind as I looked at that picture were bluntly cruel. Stupid. Retarded. Imbecile. Fool. Moron. Before that day, I would never have admitted, even to myself, that I ever thought such words about actual people. Now I was thinking them about a being who was not yet separate from me. *I was a child on the cover of that book,* and the horror of it was almost more than I could bear.

I finished paying for the book and rushed into the small elevator that went from the third-floor textbook section to ground level. The elevator was barely big enough for two slender people, and in my condition I pretty much filled it. I waited until it was between floors, then hit the stop button with a closed fist. I hit it much harder than necessary. Then I leaned back against the wall and covered my face with my hands, trying to control myself. I felt as though some evil ogre had killed my "real" baby—the baby I'd been expecting—and replaced him with an ugly, broken replica. My grief at losing that "real" baby was as intense as if he had been two years old, or five, or ten. The whole thing seemed wildly unfair to me: my baby was dead, and I was still pregnant. I was suddenly seized by a rage so strong I wanted to bash in the elevator walls.

Somewhere above the anger, my intellect registered all of this, reviewing the emotional stages of accepting a loss. First there was denial, I knew, then grief, then anger, then bargaining—no, wait, it was bargaining, then grief, then anger—or maybe anger, then bargaining, then grief? It felt as though all of them were assaulting me at once. I remembered that the final stage was acceptance. But then again, that was when the tragedy was death. What if it wasn't? What if the tragedy was born alive? I tried to force myself to reach acceptance immediately, right there in the elevator, without wading into the morass of pain I could sense just ahead of me. I considered abortion again, but the pain that lay in that direction was even greater. It was easier for me—not better, mind you, not braver or nobler or morally superior, but *easier*—to have the baby. I wondered why the psychological stages of loss didn't include fear. Maybe it was because fear pervades and overwhelms everything else. I mashed my hands against my eyes and shook so hard that the elevator compartment trembled on its cable.

From here, ten years in the future, it seems ironically fitting that I locked myself, alone, into a cramped, cold, hard, barren space near the Coop's textbook section before I let myself feel my deep emotional reaction to Adam's diagnosis. For a few of my Harvard years, I taught drawing to architecture students, and during that time I became convinced that we human beings gravitate toward spaces that are metaphors for our inner lives. That elevator pretty much summed up the way I had learned to exist. I went into it in order to gain control, an effort that had consumed me for years. It worked fairly well. After only a few seconds, before anyone could hear the alarm and come to help, I punched the button again and proceeded to the ground floor. By the time the door slid open, I had stopped crying. I would not lose control of myself in public again for some time—definitely not when I went to see Judy Trenton, to find out just how many things were likely to be wrong with the unseen person I carried under my heart.

It was between the Coop and the clinic that I passed the homeless man who looked at my abdomen and said, "Congratulations Mamma!" I glanced around, not realizing at first that he had been talking to me. I had already stopped believing that my pregnancy merited congratulations. If that man only knew, I thought bitterly. Now the memory makes me smile. I like to think that the homeless man may have been acting under the influence of the Bunraku puppeteers. Maybe he was one of them. I have a hunch that if he had known everything about my retarded baby, he would have congratulated me just as warmly. In my mind, I pictured him showing the same astonished delight I saw in Adam on the Christmas morning when he unwrapped his batteries. This little boy may not look like what you asked for, the man might have told me. He may not have the features you requested, or be able to perform all the tricks. But put him in place, and he will light up your life. You have no idea how much magic is in him.

Barry Lopez

Children in the Woods

When I was a child growing up in the San Fernando Valley in
California, a trip into Los Angeles was special. The sensation
of movement from a rural area into an urban one was sharp. On
one of these charged occasions, walking down a sidewalk with my
mother, I stopped suddenly, caught by a pattern of sunlight trapped
in a spiraling imperfection in a windowpane. A stranger, an elderly
woman in a cloth coat and a dark hat, spoke out spontaneously, saying how remarkable it is that children notice these things.

I have never forgotten the texture of this incident. Whenever
I recall it I am moved not so much by any sense of my young self
but by a sense of responsibility toward children, knowing how
acutely I was affected in that moment by that woman's words.
The effect, for all I know, has lasted a lifetime.

Now, years later, I live in a rain forest in western Oregon, on the
banks of a mountain river in relatively undisturbed country, surrounded by 150-foot-tall Douglas firs, delicate deer-head orchids,
and clearings where wild berries grow. White-footed mice and
mule deer, mink and coyote move through here. My wife and I
do not have children, but children we know, or children whose
parents we are close to, are often here. They always want to go
into the woods. And I wonder what to tell them.

In the beginning, years ago, I think I said too much. I spoke
with an encyclopedic knowledge of the names of plants or the

names of birds passing through in season. Gradually I came to say less. After a while the only words I spoke, beyond answering a question or calling attention quickly to the slight difference between a sprig of red cedar and a sprig of incense cedar, were to elucidate single objects.

I remember once finding a fragment of a raccoon's jaw in an alder thicket. I sat down alongside the two children with me and encouraged them to find out who this was—with only the three teeth still intact in a piece of the animal's maxilla to guide them. The teeth told by their shape and placement what this animal ate. By a kind of visual extrapolation its size became clear. There were other clues, immediately present, which told, with what I could add of climate and terrain, how this animal lived, how its broken jaw came to be lying here. Raccoon, they surmised. And tiny tooth marks along the bone's broken edge told of a mouse's hunger for calcium.

We set the jaw back and went on.

If I had known more about raccoons, finer points of osteology, we might have guessed more: say, whether it was male or female. But what we deduced was all we needed. Hours later, the maxilla, lost behind us in the detritus of the forest floor, continued to effervesce. It was tied faintly to all else we spoke of that afternoon.

In speaking with children who might one day take a permanent interest in natural history—as writers, as scientists, as filmmakers, as anthropologists—I have sensed that an extrapolation from a single fragment of the whole is the most invigorating experience I can share with them. I think children know that nearly anyone can learn the names of things; the impression made on them at this level is fleeting. What takes a lifetime to learn, they comprehend, is the existence and substance of myriad relationships: it is these relationships, not the things themselves, that ultimately hold the human imagination.

The brightest children, it has often struck me, are fascinated by metaphor—with what is shown in the set of relationships bearing on the raccoon, for example, to lie quite beyond the raccoon.

In the end, you are trying to make clear to them that everything found at the edge of one's senses—the high note of the winter wren, the thick perfume of propolis that drifts downwind from spring willows, the brightness of wood chips scattered by a beaver —that all this fits together. The indestructibility of these associations conveys a sense of permanence that nurtures the heart, that cripples one of the most insidious of human anxieties, the one that says, you do not belong here, you are unnecessary.

Whenever I walk with a child, I think how much I have seen disappear in my own life. What will there be for this person when he is my age? If he senses something ineffable in the landscape, will I know enough to encourage it?—to somehow show him that, yes, when people talk about violent death, spiritual exhilaration, compassion, futility, final causes, they are drawing on forty thousand years of human meditation on this—as we embrace Douglas firs, or stand by a river across whose undulating back we skip stones, or dig out a camas bulb, biting down into a taste so much wilder than last night's potatoes.

The most moving look I ever saw from a child in the woods was on a mud bar by the footprints of a heron. We were on our knees, making handprints beside the footprints. You could feel the creek vibrating in the silt and sand. The sun beat down heavily on our hair. Our shoes were soaking wet. The look said: I did not know until now that I needed someone much older to confirm this, the feeling I have of life here. I can now grow older, knowing it need never be lost.

The quickest door to open in the woods for a child is the one that leads to the smallest room, by knowing the name each thing is called. The door that leads to the cathedral is marked by a hesitancy to speak at all, rather to encourage by example a sharpness of the senses. If one speaks it should only be to say, as well as one can, how wonderfully all this fits together, to indicate what a long, fierce peace can derive from this knowledge.

Palsy

L ater, two children will dance. Others, raggedly arranged in the humid auditorium, will hula, sway, smile recklessly, clap, but only two children will dance. Wearing electric wheels for legs, they will draw arcs across the floor and open and close their own parentheses. They will do-si and—do, their stemlike necks bending with each change in direction. He will breathe from a shallow place and bow. She will put one thread of a finger into the air and spin, and spin, and this is the center of the story, this is its heart: the grace of palsy in an afternoon dance.

We do not expect what we find. We arrive with our own purpose and preoccupations, and we come early; it is that kind of show. Everyone assembled here in the wood-floored, white-walled auditorium is tied by an invisible string to a child backstage, and there is an order to things, the familiar courtesies of strangers. I have come with my mother. I have come for my son. He turns seven today, a lucky number.

Back there somewhere, Jeremy is rehearsing with his tribe: a little hula, a little shuffle, a little moment for the stage. Who would have thought it? Who would have guessed it five years ago, when we received the diagnosis? In the simmering noise of the crowd, my thoughts slide and slide backward, then pull themselves forward; occasionally, I speak to my mother. "It's crowded,"

I say. "I know that person," I say, pointing. "See the redhead? She drives a hot pink Seville." It's noise between my thoughts, and it's making me dizzy, but I feel that I owe my mother a brush of conversation, and this is all that I have in me today. "Mom," I finally confide. "About Jeremy…" I begin. And my mother says, "Please. Please. He'll be fine."

I know that he will be. I know that he is. Jeremy is fine now, but life is fragile, and who can make predictions about what will happen when a curtain is drawn—when the velvet pulls away and the child, now reaching seven, appears at last upon stage. "There are a lot of people here, Mom," I say. I worry about Jeremy and his fear of crowds. "What matters is that Jeremy's here," my mother answers. Everything else is extra.

The room fills. Seated in the front row, we feel the pressure building behind us. We are aware of movement on the periphery, of mothers sitting against the walls because there are now no chairs, of ladies' skirts drawn tight as tents across the knobs of knees. We are aware of cameras being bolted to their tripods, of siblings getting out of hand, of society knitting itself into a warm plaid fabric. "Mom," I say. "What if he can't do it? Or what if he can, and won't?" "He has always come through," my mother says, and then she fans her face with the Hula Dance program.

It is true, I think. At every fork in Jeremy's journey, he has made a choice, and he's pulled through. Acquiring speech. Acquiring strength. Acquiring rhythm. Acquiring access. Freeing his heart through his words—simple phrases without which I would not have survived: *I love you, Mommy. How are you, Mommy? Did you do anything special today?*

We are aware of hushing. We are aware of one young adult male slopping around in flip-flops as he moves between the unclipped hedges of the center aisle and toward the clearing up front. His Hawaiian shirt is neon green and desperate yellow. The piece of gold in his left ear is a hoop. The little girl at his side stands as tall as his shoulder, wearing a well-wrapped pink sheet that explodes—we hear it popping—with the catalytic fire of bright white threads. As if to guard them from the bulging audience, a phalanx of square-shouldered counselors now arrive—strong young women who convey, by their gestures, that anything is possible. She muscles the lights. She commands the canned music. She uncrumples a list from her fist and points a finger. She gestures boldly with her hands and her hands become mops, and without ever touching the overflowing floor, she has managed the spills: toes, cameras, babies all retract.

One is aware of this. One knows that now, during the final preparations, for the Hula Dance extravaganza, we—the audience, the parents, the siblings, the glass-eyed cameras, my mother, myself—must release ourselves into the care of counselors and children. The room begins to slouch like a wave being turned back to sea. I lose my equilibrium, and when I close my eyes, I see that my mind is busy separating itself into angular shades of gray. It's the beginning of a migraine, and I have never been able to explain it, but at times like these, it happens.

The truth is that I can no longer explain most things, nor can I make them any better with my words. How haunting this is: for a writer, for a mother, for a person in the world. *Jeremy*, I have said more times than one could count, *I love you. I love you. You fill my heart.* But there is nothing in those words about the way I deeply feel. About how Jeremy has taken me through these last seven years of life and taught me wonder. He has completed me—wrenched me in and out of myself, forced me past my boundaries, looked into me with his wide chocolate eyes, and demanded loyalty, spirituality, and faith. *I'm not letting you down*, he has proven over and over, and he has elevated me so that I can stand and look up and see who he is and who I must somehow be, to be his mother. I cannot explain this. I cannot put language around it, but Jeremy with his tinge of disability and his one gigantic heart, has brought me here, today, where I sit beside my mother, loving my son so absolutely and speechlessly, and still, still afraid of what will happen on the stage.

Behind me, I sense the room breathing and humming. I know that the curtain will soon rise, and I know that when I open my eyes I will no longer see the gray angles of my migraine, but crisp, jagging flashes of hot pain instead. I will focus my vision after that, and hold one hand over my left eye so that the stage will come into view. But for now I remain in the space of gray angles. My mind bobs on the surface of itself; there are collisions. Somewhere outside this gray, my mother is sitting, fanning herself with the Hula Dance program, and I would like to reach her with words, but it's impossible. The only stories that come to mind are stories about other mothers, conversations I've had. Frozen moments when I have, for example, stood in a neighbor's backyard, and stood, and helplessly listened to a sadness that slowly formed itself in words. "Two babies," this neighbor told me. "Two boys. Two children that I carry here, inside of me. And one will live and one, a genetic complication, will not. And what I want," this neighbor told me, "and what I want, I really want, is to hold both babies in my arms and bring them home and to tell them, for all of time, how much they're loved." *Words*, she said, *I will give my two sons words. For as long as God will keep them on this earth.*

Now the noise in the room is less than the silence. I open one eye and see that the capable counselors are crouched on the floor and the parents with the cameras are poised to film. Even the siblings have been brought into line, and the young man and the little girl at the front of the room exchange a few final, whispered vows in anticipation of the curtain that will soon lift from the ground. "They're getting ready to go," my mother leans over to tell me, and I draw in one long, arrhythmic breath, and slouch, at last, into my nubby plastic chair.

"Ladies and gentlemen," the little girl begins. "We are so pleased that you have come to see our show."

"It's full of talent," the young man answers. "It's full of stars."

"And we would not be here today," the little girl tells us, "were it not for the hard work of the Day Camp youngsters."

"Who have been practicing all week…"

"Who have made their very own costumes…"

"So sit back."

"You must relax."

"Listen closely for the sound of congo drums."

The audience rises to attention, and now we all lean out of our slouches and fall forward, toward the stage—my hand on my eye, my mother's program in her lap. A tinny, one-speaker version of a calypso song jiggles through the atmosphere and begins to rock the room. The young man and the child announcer step aside, encourage all eyes forward. The curtain begins its creak to heaven, and all anyone can see at first are the tiny sneakers and the knotted socks and the sometimes sandals; there's a hint of painted toes. There are forty feet on the stage and some are better clad than others, and some are tapping, and some are still rehearsing the shuffle right, the shuffle left, the tap the toes, the jump, the smack, smack, smack, the swivel on the heels.

And the Belafonte impostor is now singing the chorus, and the curtain keeps ascending, and twenty happy, anxious pairs of feet crook and stomp, and now we the audience make acquaintance with the props: floppy paper fish that curl beneath the weight of excess poster paint; hairy cardboard palm trees, their colors drying; a boat that's bobbing buoyesque; a dozen plastic leis strewn like confetti on the floor. We've been transported. We clap. We roar. Bolt upright now in our plastic chairs, we connect ankles to knees to twisted hip, to glossy faces. The wheeze and pop of exultation goes off around the room like camera lights.

In their ragged line, the children torque their way forward, arms punched to the left, to the right, chins deliberately wagging, rhythms far exceeding whatever this Belafonte mimic can deliver. This is the show, and we wag with it, taking our direction from the children, too bungled by noise and atmosphere to begin to break the whole into its parts. "Mom?" I half whisper, half scream. "Do you see him?" But it's too late to ask or answer that question, because now, halfway between the nether of the background and the edge of the sea, the children hush one another and, remembering something, suddenly, expectantly, stare off into the wings. Our eyes follow their eyes, take their cue.

They come from opposite directions—the girl and the boy in their chairs. Her gold hair susurrates around her face. His eyes, two pools of dark liquid, are as huge and as gentle as a fawn's. Their skin is the same unnamable aspect of white, and everything is loose and fragile about them but their hands, their fingers, which cling to the controls of their chairs and propel their bodies across the stage. It is enough for us that these children have appeared, but now they begin to dance, whirring in and out of each other's paths like bright tropical birds. I need both of my eyes to see this, and I bring my hand to my lap, but still it is a mystery, it is beyond human, how these two children in their crumple of bones glide and circle each other and spin, their wheels making no noises as they turn, their faces shy, soft as feathers, and triumphant.

We do not speak to one another. We do not lean over and say, *But they are tiny. But they are fragile.* We only watch them, and now we lift our eyes and watch the twenty who stand behind the two children on wheels, the twenty, Jeremy among them, who are upright as props and smiling, beaming, proud of all they can do, of who they can be on that stage—despite genetics, despite diagnoses, despite haphazard labels, despite whatever legacies their swaying shoulders bear. We, here in our plastic chairs, cannot reach out and we cannot touch; it is impossible to hold on to this beauty. We are forced to sit and to see that life is sacred and secret, and we are forced to understand these things without the tendril of touch or the logic of words. We are elevated to the courage of mothers and of fathers, to the courage of children everywhere.

Struggles with Love

"Oh, how slight the difference between 'independent' and 'ornery.'"

— BARBARA KINGSOLVER

Gerald Early

The Driving Lesson

About eighteen months ago, I taught my oldest teenage daughter how to drive. It was at the same time that I read to both my daughters J.D. Salinger's *Catcher in the Rye*, which I did largely because I was teaching it to a class, and I thought my children would be interested in a book about growing up absurd, so to speak. Not to say that I was trying to rear them that way. Naturally, I had not thought that a book about an upper-class, White teenage boy written in the late 1940s would be especially relevant. I always assume that people should be interested in learning about two things: themselves and everything that is not themselves.

Teaching Linnet how to drive is, I firmly believe, one of the great accomplishments of my life as a parent, not because it was difficult, although it had its challenging moments, but because I learned a great deal about myself and about my daughter, as well. And even this *Catcher in the Rye* business turned out to be more useful than it seemed at first.

When my daughter turned fifteen and a half, she applied for and received her learner's permit. She had thought of little else since she turned fifteen except learning how to drive. It meant a great deal to her, which struck me, at the time, as odd. When I was her age, I did not know how to drive, and did not apply for a learner's permit to take driver's education at my high school, as I thought it would do me very little good. My mother was too poor to own a car. Besides, she did not know how to drive and I lived in the middle of South Philadelphia, where public transportation was readily available and in many instances more convenient than owning a car. (Where in heaven's name could you park it?) My oldest sister, who has lived in Philadelphia most of her life, still does not know how to drive. But my daughter was living in decidedly different circumstances, in a two-car, middle-class family, and in a suburb where public transportation is sporadic and far from convenient. It certainly doesn't take you anywhere you want to go. In a sense, she understood very rightly that if she were to have a period of her adolescence independent of her parents, she needed to learn to drive. She told me this in no uncertain terms and cut me short when I began to reminisce about growing up in Philadelphia. "I'm not growing up in some cold-water, coal-burning flat in an inner-city neighborhood. I'm not living your childhood and I don't care about it." Well, that's telling me, I thought.

My wife had given Linnet her first driving lesson and came back entirely bemused and out of sorts. Linnet came in crying, marched upstairs, and slammed the door to her room.

"I can't teach that girl to drive," my wife said. "She scares me too much behind a wheel. Why don't you take her out? You're much better at teaching than I am. Remember, you taught me how to drive. Besides, this is something a father should do with his daughter."

My wife was exaggerating for effect and because she wanted to get out of something she found disagreeable. I had not really taught her how to drive. When we began dating, she owned a Nova, a new car at the time with an automatic transmission, and I was driving my mother's Toyota, a somewhat less-than-new car with a standard transmission. She expressed an interest in wanting to learn how to drive a car with a standard transmission, so I taught her. As my wife is a very good driver, and she did, after all, already know how to drive, it was easy to teach her, and I think she was driving my mother's car on the street in a matter of two or three days. For the first ten years of our marriage, we owned nothing but standard transmission cars. And she thought I was the greatest teacher in the world because I was so relaxed and patient, was never the least concerned that she couldn't master the stick shift, was never upset when she made a mistake, and explained things thoroughly and clearly. This was all an act. I was terrified to my toenails the whole time, but I suspected that she thought that, as a man, I should exhibit a certain coolness.

The one prolonged teaching session I had with my mother was when she taught me to drive when I was eighteen. My mother had learned to drive only two years earlier, and she seemed very keen that I should learn as well. I don't remember having much enthusiasm for it. To this day, I hate to drive. What compounded my situation was that my mother's car had a manual transmission. The lessons were tense. My mother was extremely nervous and extremely angry, although I picked up driving with relative ease. She kept thinking I would strip the gears, run into something, or get run into, normal fears but in her case pitched at high frequency.

After three lessons, I could drive the car, a Volkswagen Beetle, fairly well. But I hated the lessons. Then, suddenly, one day, she decided to have a male friend continue the instruction. The change was dramatic. He was very laid-back, patient, and had endless confidence, or pretended confidence, in my ability. The lessons were no longer an ordeal. I learned two things from this switch, which I think in part my mother effected because she wanted me to receive instruction from a man. First, I decided I wanted very much to teach people things in the manner of a middle-aged Black man, because I thought all middle-aged Black men taught like my new driving instructor, and all of my life, I have associated good teaching with being middle-aged, Black, and a man. I wanted to be patient, assured, relaxed, with boundless confidence in my student and in my ability to teach him or her. Second, paradoxically, is that I missed my mother as an instructor. I thought there was something in this cross-gender moment of instruction that helped me understand what being a man was. Perhaps this is why my wife was able, very easily, to talk me into teaching my daughter how to drive. "Men are better teachers at mechanical things than women are," my wife told me in an appeal to my ego. I don't believe it. I am the most hapless man with mechanical contrivances that I know. But it meant something to my male ego to teach my daughter to drive, especially because my wife felt unable to do it.

I went upstairs and talked to Linnet.

"Didn't go too well today, huh?" I asked.

"Daddy," she turned to me with her tear-streaked face, "teach me how to drive. Mommy thinks I can't do it. I know I can learn to drive if you teach me. I think you're the best teacher in the world. Remember how you taught me to play checkers and Monopoly and stuff like that. You always explain stuff well and never get mad if I need to have it explained again. I think most of the stuff I remember you taught me."

It is a terrible weight put on any parent to hear that suddenly and so sincerely from a child, as if the dreadful responsibility of childrearing appears in such vivid relief at such a moment.

I have been a terrible parent, I thought. This kid can't believe what she is saying. Immediately, it struck me that the last thing I wanted to do was teach my daughter to drive. I felt dizzy from the sheer immensity of it, as if, in some surreal moment, I was assigned to teach her the most important task a human being ever could be taught and feeling myself insufficient for the undertaking. After all, I secretly thought that perhaps because of a learning disability, Linnet couldn't learn how to drive. I remember trying to dissuade her from getting her learner's permit, telling her there was "no rush," that she had plenty of time. "You don't know how much time I have," she responded angrily. "Driving isn't everything," I would tell her at other times. "It is to me," she would answer. I felt like a fraud bearing a sickening guilt.

"I'll teach you how to drive," I said.

We went out early every Sunday during early spring. We would drive around the huge empty parking lot on the Washington University campus in St. Louis for about an hour. Turn left. Turn right.

Pull into a parking stall. Keep the car straight. Keep your eyes on the road. Check your rearview mirror. The usual instructions. I was calm, collected, coolly explaining everything and giving her tips about various complications that could arise when she actually would drive in traffic, which I promised her week after week but always found some excuse not to fulfill. So, she wound up driving around the parking lot for far longer than most drivers-ed students. After a bit, she wanted to drive on the street, but she never became impatient about it, believing that her father knew best.

One very cold, very sunny Sunday, I decided to have her drive from one parking lot to another. This involved going up a winding, tricky stretch of road. I thought she could handle it. We went up without too much difficulty. But when we returned, matters became very dicey very quickly. Going down the winding road meant hugging a high brick wall that abutted the road. The car started going faster than Linnet could control, the nearness of the wall unnerved her, and she couldn't keep the car straight. She turned the steering wheel and it seemed we were going to hit the wall. Maybe she had better control of the car than I thought. Maybe she wasn't going to hit the wall. Until that point, I had been, against my inner urges, very cool, but when I thought she was going to hit the wall, I panicked and grabbed the wheel.

"Goddamnit," I yelled, "you're going to get us killed."

I pushed her out of the way and guided the car down the road, virtually sitting on top of her. When we reached the bottom of the hill, I stopped the car.

"Look," I said, a bit sheepishly, "I'm sorry about that, but it looked like you were about to…"

Her head was down. She was crying quietly.

"I wasn't going to crash into the wall," she said. "You don't think I can learn how to drive, do you? You never did. You think I'm too dumb to learn to drive, don't you?"

I was silent for a moment. I didn't quite know what to say. I stammered something, but she wasn't listening. She got out of the car and opened the door on the passenger side.

"I guess you better drive us home," she said.

"Listen, Linnet, I'm sorry. I didn't mean…"

"Drive," she yelled at me. I was so startled that I simply obeyed her and got behind the wheel.

I started the car, but I didn't move it. I was trying to formulate something to say, an apology of some sort. I felt so exposed. She knew she had hit a nerve when she said I did not think she could learn to drive. But before I could say anything, she spoke to me in a quiet, choked voice, wiping her face with the heel of her hand.

"Do you know I got out of the Resource Room this year?" she said.

"Yes," I said, "I know that. That's very good for you."

"Hardly any kid gets out of Resource," she said, ignoring my interjection. "Once you get in special education, you stay there. And everybody thinks you're dumb. Even the teachers think you're dumb and they don't help you. They just do the work for you. It's awful to have everybody think you're dumb. I wanted to get out of there so bad. I worked and worked and got out. I'm not dumb, and I was tired of people thinking I was dumb."

"I never thought you were dumb, Linnet," I said.

"You know, there are a lot of Black kids in Resource. I didn't want to be there because I thought, everybody will think I'm dumb because I'm Black."

This was becoming too painful. What goes on in the minds of children is something adults don't want to know about. I didn't want to hear anymore. What was I supposed to say, some trite, unconvincing thing about your great Black ancestry, the wonders of Africa? People who think those recitations make a difference are afraid to plumb the awful and contradictory depths of the human soul. There was no escaping racial pride, in the end, as that was what motivated her to get out of the Resource Room. And there was no escaping race as a burden, a stigma, a form of shame. A Black person is forever caught between a kind of heroism and simply being the nigger. I pressed the accelerator.

"We don't have to go through this now, Linnet," I said.

"It's hard to go to school. A lot of the White kids are racist and can't stand most of the Black kids. And most of the Blacks think you're a sellout if you have White friends, and they go around in some kind of clan. They think like their parents. All of them do. I don't want to like something just to make the Black kids happy, make them think I'm Black. They say I act White, but I'm just trying to be myself. What is this being Black? Hanging around complaining about White people all the time. Thinking about your color all the time and how different you're supposed to be? Just being part of a clan? But a lot of White kids do dope, come from messed-up homes, and just act crazy. I don't act like that. I sure don't want to be White. I want to be myself. That's why I wanted to learn to drive. To help me be myself," she said.

I had driven a few blocks but pulled the car over. I looked at my daughter for a moment and realized that God does indeed give only ironic gifts.

"You know something?" Linnet continued, "I kind of liked the *Catcher in the Rye*. I mean, some of it. But Holden Caulfield was just too crazy. Sometimes I think he's right, though. I think sometimes everybody in the world is phony. I know I think the Black kids and their blackness and the White kids and their whiteness are all phony. They just don't know how to be themselves."

I got out of the car and went around to the passenger side, opened the door and shoved her gently toward the driver's seat.

"I don't feel like driving," I said.

"I don't want to do this, Daddy," she said. She was now completely in the driver's seat.

"Then, I guess, we're not getting home, because I'm not driving," I said.

"I might mess up the car, "she said.

"I'll buy another one and take you out next week. There are plenty of car dealers around. Buying another car is easy. As Hemingway said, the world is 'a good place to buy in.' Go ahead and drive."

Anne Lamott

Ashes

A sh Wednesday came early this year. It is supposed to be about preparation, about consecration, about moving toward Easter, toward resurrection and renewal. It offers us a chance to break through the distractions that keep us from living the basic Easter message of love, of living in wonder rather than doubt. For some people, it is about fasting, to symbolize both solidarity with the hungry and the hunger for God. (I, on the other hand, am not heavily into fasting; the thought of missing even a single meal sends me running in search of Ben and Jerry's Mint Oreo.)

So there are many ways to honor the day, but as far as I know, there is nothing in Scripture or tradition setting it aside as the day on which to attack one's child and then to flagellate oneself while the child climbs a tree and shouts down that he can't decide whether to hang himself or jump, even after it is pointed out nicely that he is only five feet from the ground.

But I guess every family celebrates in its own unique way.

Let me start over. You see, I tried at breakfast to get Sam interested in Ash Wednesday. I made him cocoa and gave a rousing talk on what it all means. We daub our foreheads with ashes, I explained, because they remind us of how much we miss and celebrate those who have already died. The ashes remind us of the finality of death. Like the theologian said, death is God's no to all human presumption. We are sometimes like the characters in *Waiting for Godot,* where the only visible redemption is the eventual appearance in Act Two of four or five new leaves on the pitiful tree. On such a stage, how can we cooperate with grace? How can we open ourselves up to it? How can we make room for anything new? How can we till the field? And so people also mark themselves with ashes to show that they trust in the alchemy God can work with those ashes—jogging us awake, moving us toward greater attention and openness and love.

Sam listened very politely to my little talk. Then when he thought I wasn't looking, he turned on the TV. I made him turn it off. I explained that in honor of Ash Wednesday we were not watching cartoons that morning. I told him he could draw if he wanted, or play with Legos. I got myself a cup of coffee and started looking at a book of photographs that someone had sent. One in particular caught my eye immediately. It was of a large Mennonite family, shot in black and white—a husband and wife and their fifteen children gathered around a highly polished oval table, their faces clearly, eerily reflected by the burnished wood. They looked surreal and serious; you saw in those long grave faces the echoes of the Last Supper. I wanted to show the photograph to Sam. But abruptly, hideously, Alvin and the Chipmunks were singing "Achy Breaky Heart" in their nasal demon-field way—on the TV that Sam had turned on again.

And I just lost my mind. I thought I might begin smashing things. Including Sam. I shouted at the top of my lungs, and I used the word *fucking*; as in "goddamn fucking TV that we're getting rid of," and I grabbed him by his pipe-cleaner arm and jerked him in the direction of his room, where he spent the next ten minutes crying bitter tears.

It's so awful, attacking your child. It is the worst thing I know, to shout loudly at this fifty-pound being with his huge trusting brown eyes. It's like bitch-slapping E.T.

I did what all good parents do: calmed down enough to go apologize, and beg for his forgiveness while simultaneously expressing a deep concern about his disappointing character.

He said I was the meanest person on earth next to Darth Vader. We talked and then he went off to his room. I chastised myself silently while washing breakfast dishes, but then it was time for school and I couldn't find him anywhere. I looked everywhere in the house, in closets, under beds, and finally I heard him shouting from the branches of our tree.

I coaxed him down, dropped him off at school, and felt terrible all day. Everywhere I went I'd see businessmen and women marching purposefully by with holy ashes on their foreheads. I couldn't go to church until that night to get my own little ash *tilak*, the reminder that I was forgiven. I thought about taking Sam out of school so that I could apologize some more. But I knew just enough to keep my mitts off him. Now, at seven, he is separating from me like mad and has made it clear that I need to give him a little bit more room. I'm not even allowed to tell him I love him these days. He is quite firm on this. "You tell me you love me all the time," he explained recently, "and I don't want you to anymore."

"At all?" I said.

"I just want you to tell me that you like me."

I said I would really try. That night, when I was tucking him in, I said, "Good night, honey. I really like you a lot."

There was silence in the dark. Then he said, "I like you too, Mom."

So I didn't take him out of school. I went for several walks, and I thought about ashes. I was sad that I am an awful person, that I am the world's meanest mother. I got sadder. And I got to thinking about the ashes of the dead.

Twice I have held the ashes of people I adored—my dad's, my friend Pammy's. Nearly twenty years ago I poured my father's into the water near Angel Island, late at night, but I was twenty-five years old and very drunk at the time and so my grief was anesthetized. When I opened the box of his ashes, I thought they would be nice and soft and, well, ashy, like the ones with which they anoint your forehead on Ash Wednesday. But they're the grittiest of elements, like not very good landscaping pebbles. As if they're made of bones or something.

I tossed a handful of Pammy's into the water way out past the Golden Gate Bridge during the day, with her husband and family, when I had been sober several years. And this time I was able to see, because it was daytime and I was sober, the deeply contradictory nature of ashes—that they are both so heavy and so light. They're impossible to let go of entirely. They stick to things, to your fingers, your sweater. I licked my friend's ashes off my hand, to taste them, to taste her, to taste what was left after all that was clean and alive had been consumed, burned away. They tasted metallic, and they blew every which way. We tried to strew them off the side of the boat romantically, with seals barking from the rocks on shore, under a true-blue sky, but they would not cooperate. They rarely will. It's frustrating if you are hoping to have a happy ending, or at least a little closure, a movie moment when you toss them into the air and they flutter and disperse. They don't. They cling, they haunt. They get in your hair, in your eyes, in your clothes.

By the time I reached into the box of Pammy's ashes, I had had Sam, so I was able to tolerate a bit more mystery and lack of order. That's one of the gifts kids give you, because after you have a child, things come out much less orderly and rational than they did before. It's so utterly bizarre to stare into the face of one of these tiny perfect beings and to understand that you (or someone a lot like you) grew them after a sweaty little bout of sex. And then, weighing in at the approximate poundage of a medium honeydew melon, they proceed to wedge open your heart. (Also, they help you see that you are as mad as a hatter, capable of violence just because Alvin and the Chipmunks are singing when you are trying to have a nice spiritual moment thinking about ashes.)By the time I held Pammy's ashes in my hand, I almost liked that they grounded me in all the sadness and mysteriousness; I could find a comfort in that. There's a kind of sweetness and attention that you can finally pay to the tiniest grains of life after you've run your hands through the ashes of someone you loved. Pammy's ashes clung to us. And so I licked them off my fingers. She was the most robust and luscious person I have ever known.

Sam went home after school with a friend, so I only saw him for a few minutes later, before he went off to dinner with his Big Brother Brian, as he does every Wednesday. I went to my church. The best part of the service was that we sang old hymns a cappella. There were only eight of us, mostly women, some black, some white, mostly well over fifty, scarves in their hair, lipstick, faces like pansies and cats. One of the older women was in a bad mood. I found this very scary, as if I were a flight attendant with one distressed passenger who wouldn't let me help. I tried to noodge her into a better mood with flattery and a barrage of questions about her job, garden, and dog, but she was having none of it.

This was discouraging at first, until I remembered another woman at our church, very old, from the South, tiny and black, who dressed in ersatz Coco Chanel outfits, polyester sweater sets, Dacron pillbox hats. They must have come from Mervyn's and Montgomery Ward because she didn't have any money. She was always cheerful—until she turned eighty and started going blind. She had a great deal of religious faith, and everyone assumed that she would adjust and find meaning in her loss—meaning and then acceptance and then joy—and we all wanted this because, let's face it, it's so inspiring and such a relief when people find a way to bear the unbearable, when you can organize things in such a way that a tiny miracle appears to have taken place and that love has once again turned out to be bigger than fear and death and blindness. But this woman would have none of it. She went into a deep depression and eventually left the church. The elders took communion to her in the afternoon on the first Sunday of the month—homemade bread and grape juice for the sacrament, and some bread to toast later—but she wouldn't be part of our community anymore. It must have been too annoying for her that everyone was trying to manipulate her into being a better sport than she was capable of being. I always thought that was heroic of her, that it spoke of such integrity to refuse to pretend you're doing well just to help other people deal with the fact that sometimes we face an impossible loss.

Still, on Ash Wednesday I sang, of faith and love, of repentance. We tore cloth rags in half to symbolize our repentance, our willingness to tear up the old pattern and await the new; we dipped our own fingers in ash and daubed it on our foreheads. I prayed for the stamina to bear mystery and stillness. I prayed for Sam to be able to trust me and for me to be able to trust me again, too.

When I got home, Sam was already asleep. Brian had put him to bed. I wanted to wake him up and tell him that it was OK that he wouldn't be who I tried to get him to be, that it was OK that he didn't cooperate with me all the time—that ashes don't, old people don't, why should little boys? But I let him alone. He was in my bed when I woke up the next morning, way over on the far left, flat and still as a shift of light. I watched him sleep. His mouth was open. Just the last few weeks, he had grown two huge front teeth, big and white as Chiclets. He was snoring loudly for such a small boy.

I thought again about that photo of the Mennonites. In the faces of those fifteen children, reflected on their dining room table, you could see the fragile ferocity of their bond: it looked like a big wind could come and blow away this field of people on the shiny polished table. And the light shining around them where they stood was so evanescent that you felt that if the reflections were to go, the children would be gone, too.

More than anything else on earth, I do not want Sam ever to blow away, but you know what? He will. His ashes will stick to the fingers of someone who loves him. Maybe his ashes will blow that person into a place where things do not come out right, where things cannot be boxed up or spackled back together but where somehow he or she can see, with whatever joy can be mustered, the four or five leaves on the formerly barren tree.

"Mom?" he called out suddenly in his sleep.

"Yes," I whispered, "here I am," and he slung his arm toward the sound of my voice, out across my shoulders.

Debra Gwartney

The End of Summer

When I picked up my four daughters at the Portland Airport during the second August after my divorce from their father, I'd already planned several outings to get them back to me. One of those had to do with berries.

Strawberry season had come around during their last week of school. The girls and I spent their last Saturday morning before their summer visitation in Arizona gathering a pail of the bright red, and still sour, nuggets at a local farm. We crawled on our hands and knees between the rows of bushes and picked until our palms and tongues were stained crimson. But the girls were long gone, already searching for fat pink cactus fruit with their father in the broiling Sonoran Desert, when the fullness of Oregon berry season hit. I watched as the outdoor market near my house turned into tables heaped with raspberries, marionberries, blueberries, loganberries, gooseberries. Berries that were the cure for rain and mist, for the gray November we'd barely made it through, for the soaked January. My kids didn't get to taste the mounds of fruit packed in leaf-green cardboard containers, the ones that sat on my refrigerator shelf through July and early August like a basket of gems.

I'd sent the girls a package of dense, dark marionberries in mid-July so they'd have a sample of the Oregon harvest they'd miss as long as the custody agreement was in force. I wrapped the berries in Styrofoam and padded bags of dry ice and then more foam. But Amanda, the oldest, called me the day the box arrived by UPS truck and said the plastic container was full of only brown mush, turned to vinegar.

By the time my daughters arrived home at the end of August the only fresh berries available were blackberries. The rebel fruit. This was a crop that grew on untamed vines far from any farmer's cultivated rows. Berries the size and color of a sore thumb that hid in bunches on the thorny, invasive weed that covered about every patch of spare land in the valley. The out-of-control tendrils wrapped around our back fence, covered empty lots downtown, and choked the hillsides of the Mt. Pisgah Arboretum, a nearby mountain where I hiked. Blackberries didn't have the delicacy of raspberries or the fresh burst of a blueberry; instead, the taste was slightly overripe—you could almost taste the future wine in it— laden with seeds, and on the verge of bitter. When you bit into a blackberry, it bit back. But at the end of summer, blackberries were abundant. And free. Tossed with a little cinnamon and sugar and topped with oatmeal, they made a good crisp. Most important, they were available the first day Amanda, Stephanie, Mary, and Mollie were home from their father's house.

Their first day back, the girls agreed that going blackberry hunting was a fine way to celebrate their homecoming. I'd suggested the outing when they were finally out of bed and standing in the kitchen like visitors wondering if it were okay to poke through the cupboards for bowls and cups. Amanda, with her thirteen-year-old long and gangly legs, said it would feel good to stretch out after the previous day's long airplane ride. I'd endure leaving behind the suitcases of dirty clothes, and the girls would leave their rooms waiting to be rediscovered and we'd take off to Mt. Pisgah, a short distance away. I let myself believe it was a wonderful plan.

That is, until an hour later when we were well up the winding trail, bordered with Douglas fir and vine maple, that would lead us to a dusty clump of berry bushes on top. The hill had become steep after the first quarter-mile and one after another the girls complained that their legs ached and their feet hurt. They were tired, hungry, bored.

"Can we go home?" Mary asked me, grinding her fist into her eye. A bug had flown into her eyelashes, and Stephanie leaned close to her to pick out the wings. It struck me that in the past her sisters would have stepped back and waited for me to take care of any such mishap, but now their attention to each other was automatic. I was standing to the side, wanting to take over but hesitating, when I noticed Amanda's stiff back and slightly jutted chin. This was too much, more than she and her sisters had counted on—wordlessly she let me know it was time to quit.

But I didn't want to quit. I was sure that once we got to the top and to the sweet fruit, all this tension among us would drop away and we'd be finally, fully reunited. I wasn't going to let leg cramps or insects thwart my intentions for a day that had been planned a long time. The hike would reimmerse my kids in the smells and winds and shadows and tastes of the Willamette Valley. It would get them out of Arizona, out of their father's world, and into mine.

I moved in then to hold Mary's face in my hand and check that her eye was clear. Then I took her hand, and one of Mollie's. "Come on," I said, pulling the two younger ones along as I took broad strides up the path, "It's not that far." Then I promised again all the bounty they could stand at the end of the trail.

That morning I'd risen at first light to make breakfast. Amanda and Stephanie were still asleep in their twin beds upstairs. Mary was buried alone in the covers of the queen-size bed she shared with her little sister in the room across from mine. Mollie, six years old, was in my bed, deep into slumber despite the morning sun streaming through the windows of our little house, casting yellow stripes across her face. She'd planted herself in that spot the night before: right in the middle of my sheets. As soon as the lights went out, about an hour after getting home from the long drive from the airport, Mollie had pattered across the wood floor and crawled in next to me without a word, pressing her knees in the small of my back. The round caps had rested against me through the night.

I made coffee thinking about how they were bone-tired, the girls, and would sleep late. I tried not to disrupt the peace, moving softly in my slippers, opening the front door quietly to get the paper. I avoided the washing machine, though I was hankering to rinse summer out of their swim suits, T-shirts, and shorts. I took the coffee grinder to the bathroom and wrapped it in a towel before I turned it on.

But the truth is, I let *some* noise escape; a few bumps and squeaks of cupboard doors, the whistle of the kettle on the stove. I already figured Amanda and Stephanie, thirteen and eleven, were going to have a tough time with the in-between days—not quite out of Arizona, not quite in Oregon—so I was glad to postpone their glumness for another hour or two. But circumstances were different with Mary and Mollie. From speaking with them on the phone while they were away, I knew how much my younger daughters wanted to be with me again. And I knew how much I wanted to be with them. I made just enough sound, I was hopeful, to stir these two out of sleep. So one would stumble out to the kitchen, rubbing her eyes, and find me at the table with a steaming mug of coffee in my hand. She'd curl in my lap, sigh, and lean into me with her fingers wrapped around my wrist. "Hold me, Mommy," she'd say.

I set my mug down with an extra-loud clunk and listened for the rustle of an awakened child.

Still, as eager as I was for one of the little girls to come out, I remember feeling disappointment at the same time. The pure joy I'd imagined for two-and-a-half months, the joy I was sure a good mother would feel without question, hadn't risen in me as I thought it would the instant I saw my daughters. My happiness was dampened for some reason; a milder version than I'd planned on. Why? All summer I'd let the idea of their return bloom like a winter camellia in my chest. I hadn't planned on experiencing any wobble of misgiving or fear. Where had that come from?

Even though I'd kept my focus on motherhood while they were gone, those ten entire weeks alone had, despite my narrow concentration, created a notion of space and time different from any I'd known since Amanda's birth. I'd claimed to hate it, that space, all summer, but now I panicked a little at its ending. It was going away quietly, instantly, as ephemeral as the steam rising from my coffee. I almost reached out to grab the sense of what it means to be alone, at least one last clear memory before it got away. But it disappeared too fast. My daughters wouldn't leave again until the end of the school year, a reality that both terrified and thrilled me. For nearly nine months they were all mine. I was all theirs.

As we moved closer to the berry patch, Amanda and Stephanie tromped up the mountain ahead of Mary and Mollie. I brought up the rear. I watched Mollie scamper over the pebbled path, dust puffing around her sneakers while she gazed at the sky, when suddenly she stumbled over an embedded boulder. Her body pitched forward and she threw her hands in front of herself to catch the fall, but her knee smacked into a sharp rock as she hit the ground. She howled and I ran up to her, lifting her onto my lap and brushing the dirt from her wound to see how bad it was. I wrapped my arms around her while she pressed her face into my shirt.

"Can we go back to the car?" she said.

"Oh, honey," I said, "You're okay. It's just a scrape." I pulled out my water bottle and squirted a stream on the dirty cut. A brownish-red trickle ran down her calf, which I wiped away with my fingers.

Mollie hadn't seen the rock, I guessed, because she'd been busy watching the sky for the bird. Before we started our hike, I'd read about it on a display board at the trailhead. The Pisgah Bird, the sign said, was brown with white pinfeathers, had a long hooked beak, and a wingspan of at least sixteen feet. Though it hadn't been spotted for more than one hundred years, it was once known to sweep down and pluck children—those who'd ventured into the exposed areas—off the side of the mountain. The only way to frighten it off was to shout its name, *Pisgah!*, as loudly as possible.

"Really?" Mollie had asked after I'd read the brief passage aloud. She reached over to take hold of my pant leg.

"Are you that dumb?" Amanda said from behind me. I turned to see her exchange an arched eyebrow with Stephanie.

"It's an old story," I said to Mollie, and to Mary, who'd stepped closer to me. "Someone made it up."

I realize now how lazy my mother instinct had become, even though I pretended it hadn't. I should have known just by glancing at the folklore on the board that it wasn't a good one to pass on to Mary and Mollie. They had enough worries on their first day home—they didn't need the threat of a big, mean bird, too. But I hadn't thought it through in time. Now the story was out, and I was obligated to beat myself up about that, too. As Mollie and I headed back up the trail, the dull guilt that had been cooking in me about the outing became sharper and hotter. Why had I made their homecoming more difficult instead of the easy, smooth afternoon I'd planned on?

Amanda and Stephanie drummed out steady complaints to reinforce that my perfect day wasn't so perfect after all. It was too dusty, they said, and grit from the trail was getting in their eyes and noses. The flies and mosquitoes bothered them. And it was too hot, Amanda said, though I reminded her that they'd left the 110-degree weather in Tucson, and here it was no more than a balmy 85.

Their crabbing continued to the base of a sharp incline, where another sign told us we were halfway up the three-mile hill. Mollie, hearing that, held up her shimmering red kneecap and pleaded with me to piggyback her up the next section. I knelt on the path so she could climb on; she settled on my back with her legs wrapped around my waist and her arms draped across my shoulders. Mary took hold of my hand, so I could pull her along as well.

"How much longer?" Mary asked, the fourth or fifth time.

"A ways," I said.

Amanda and Stephanie, lagging behind, whispered to each other about sneaking back to the car, just loud enough that I could hear.

I try to remember, exactly, why I'd thought the hike would help us. Why hadn't I known it was too soon to drag the girls to the mountain? They would have been happier in their rooms, reminiscing with each other about the summer, drifting through memories of Arizona, telling stories about their dad they'd try not to recite in my presence. They'd have been relieved to be near a phone, so they could call him a couple of times and not feel so suddenly cut off from his presence. But there was something in me that day that wouldn't allow us to go back. I wanted desperately for the girls to return to this part of the world, the one that was their own with me. I wanted them to touch it, to drink it, to eat it. To forget about him.

On the cusp of September, the blackberry bushes I'd spotted during a few summer hikes had to be bursting with plump purple fruit. I was sure of it. The weekends I'd hiked up the winding path alone, I'd stood on top and gazed at the panoramic view of our city and imagined my girls up there gathering juicy pails of berries. We'd transform the fruit into pies and crisps and cobblers, or sprinkle them across our cereal in the morning. I'd dreamed of the day a hundred times, how simple it would be among us. But the real afternoon wasn't like that at all. The older girls banged the empty sand buckets we'd dug from the toybox against their skinny legs. Stephanie told Mary to get lost, to stop following so close. She accused Mollie of backwashing in the water jug and of hogging the graham crackers. I pulled out some cheddar slices I'd wrapped in plastic, but Amanda spoke for the lot of them: Didn't

I know? Over the summer they decided they hated warm, sweaty cheese.

Mollie's arms tightened around my neck until my throat felt crowded. I bent my knees to slide her off. "Walk a while," I said, but she didn't move and instead held out her arms. "Carry me!" she cried in an old baby voice. I scooped her up from her under-arms until her thin body eased into mine. Though I'd held her several times since she'd been back, it struck me in that moment how much she'd grown over the summer. She was heavier than she had been in June, and longer. I folded my arms around her, feeling for the parts that were new to me, a bit of skin, an inch of hair. I reached down to touch the top of Mary's head, then, real-izing that she too was bigger. This eight-year-old daughter came past my hips now, her arms and legs lankier and her shoulders shed of the last ounces of baby fat.

Amanda trudged past, growling at her little sisters and at me for being in the way. It didn't even occur to me to pull Amanda into the embrace, or Stephanie for that matter. What kind of mother was I to miss a chance to hug them? Why had I let them go by without even trying? I didn't call to them or try to catch up with them, though I should have, but swung Mollie to my back while Mary's arm snaked around my leg. I watched Amanda and Stephanie, straight and thin as matchsticks, march toward the open meadow at the top of the mountain and pushed the brewing guilt away. The thorned bushes ahead, laden with fruit, would put them in a better mood. At least that's what I promised myself: that the berry gathering would finally bring us together.

I could have done a better job over the summer preparing for coolness from Amanda; it was inevitable because of her age and the weeks she'd spent with her father. But I hadn't even consid-ered that she'd return with tenuousness instead of utter glee, so, as lousy as it sounds now, I instantly reacted to her distance with distance. Maybe she'd warm to me again; maybe she wouldn't, I didn't know. She was days from starting the eighth grade; the troubled look that now and then drifted across her face told how scared she was about the last part of middle school. She'd been the new kid the year before and it had taken her until spring to make friends. On the verge of finally being accepted by a small group of girls, she was off for a summer in Tucson. She was sure, she'd told me after we were home from the airport and I'd asked if she was going to call her pals, that they'd spent the warm months swimming and having sleepovers and talking on the phone and forgetting about her. I sat down on her bed when she revealed this. I believed in that moment that she'd signaled an opening, a place for me to step in. I reached for her hand, but she pulled away, slightly but unmistakably, burrowing into her bedcovers.

"I know how hard this is," I said, folding my own hands in my lap.

She looked up at me from her pillow, stared hard with steel-gray eyes, her straight blond hair tucked like a curtain around her narrow face. "No you don't," she said.

Stephanie sat up at the sound in Amanda's voice and moved from her own bed across the room. She slid in next to her big sister and draped one arm around Amanda's waist. Stephanie looked at me as if she were pleading for peace, for an ease that would come only after I left. Or at least that's what I took from her—that she was asking me to fade back, to get out of their way. They stayed still and wrapped in each other, my oldest children, the room full of their breath and mine. At that moment, I could have laid down, too, seizing a piece of the narrow bed for my body and throwing an arm around both girls. But I stood and muttered that I loved them before I switched off the light and went downstairs to find Mary and Mollie.

When we finally reached the top of Mt. Pisgah and the girls saw the bushes that I'd described on the way up, Amanda and Stephanie chose a thick bush at the edge of the clearing while Mary, Mollie, and I staked out another. It was only a matter of seconds before I realized how ridiculous it had been to think the picking at the end of the hike would be a good thing. It was impossible for the younger girls to thrust their hands into a cluster of dangling berries without getting gouged and scratched. The vines were alive, pinching Mary's thighs, pinning Mollie's shoulder. Stephanie yelled for me when her long hair got tangled in the mass of thorns. I jogged across the field to pluck her free, stabbing my fingers and forearms. The handful of berries that managed to get into the buckets was hardly worth this trouble: the climb uphill, the mass of barbed stickers, the angled sun that stung our eyes. Amanda was yelling at Mary, and Mollie was sniffling and lowering herself to the dusty ground. Our first outing of our year together, the one I'd pictured so many times in the weeks before they'd come home, was a bust. The connection I wanted to come out of the ground, from the sky, from the trees, and the air—the welcoming soil that would root my daughters back in their place—refused to appear.

Amanda stretched out on the stubby grass, yellow and brittle after months without rain, and Stephanie plopped next to her. I went around to the other side of the bush to pick fast before one or the other rose yet another clamor to go back to the car. My determination had shifted: now I meant to collect enough fruit to combine with what the girls had gathered for at least a cobbler. That night, when cool air that hinted of fall drifted in through our windows and Mary and Mollie were fresh and pink from the bathtub, I'd set a warm dessert in front of my daughters and scoop ice cream on top. Thick and bubbling and homemade. Something I could give them that no one else could. Something that tasted exactly like home.

I came back around the thicket, my bucket half full, to see that Mary and Mollie, too, had wandered over to sit with their big sisters. The younger girls were giggling, leaning in to watch as Amanda smashed berries into a small puddle in her palm and then, with her index finger, drew wide streaks across Stephanie's cheeks. I couldn't hold back my irritation: How dare she waste the fruit like that? Afraid that I'd start yelling at her if I didn't move away, I returned to picking. I thrust my arm far into the dark nest to get the hidden berries, the ripest, the juiciest, and the most elusive. I buried myself in the thorns and leaves, yearning desperately to be alone—the very state I'd despised the day before. But I couldn't be alone anymore; I couldn't even block the sound of laughter from those who were dependent upon me outside my shadowed perch.

In ten minutes I had nearly enough in my pail to fill a pie pan. My fingers were sticky and hot and the color of a fresh bruise. I pulled myself free of the vines and headed toward my cluster of daughters. The girls had moved from the open area to a shady spot of grass. They sat under a giant maple tree and its dappled, comforting rustle of green star leaves. When I got near enough, I realized that Amanda had emptied her sisters' pots of every berry. And I saw why. She'd crushed the fruit and used the mash to paint all the girls' faces. Mary, Mollie, and Stephanie were purple, forehead to chin. Amanda had covered her own face, as well—and her hands were almost black from the dark fruit. Mollie's eyelashes were caked with seeds; juice ran down Stephanie's white neck and onto her T-shirt; strands of Mary's waist-long hair were now the color of distant clouds seconds before the sun disappears. The pails—red and green and blue—were tossed aside, blown about by a breeze coming over the top of the mountain. From a few yards away, I stared at my daughters. I didn't know what to say. They hadn't yet noticed me; they were that intent on watching Amanda put the last touches on Stephanie, covering every tiny inch of pale skin to the earlobes. The girls squeezed in next to each other. Four purple beads on a tight string.

I heard laughter behind me and turned to see two women coming off the trail and into the clearing. "My goodness!" one of them said, pointing past me. Both women chuckled, as did several others who climbed up behind them. A small audience formed. My purple daughters glanced up, three gleaming at the attention from strangers. Mollie called out to me, "Mommy!" But I stayed still, my eyes on Amanda. I'd noticed that when the strangers laughed she moved away, turning her back against the crowd. That wasn't enough, though—she scooted behind Stephanie so her body wouldn't show. She made a huddle of herself behind her wall of sisters.

Something powerful could have happened in that moment—I feel the potential of it even now, looking back from the other end of a decade. I remember the swell of my heart toward Amanda as I recognized her impulse to hide herself, then hide herself again. What was she trying to tell me that afternoon on top of the hill? Maybe she was asking me to back off, to let them come home in their own time. Maybe she was letting me know that for a period of days or weeks during the transition she, not I, would be her sisters' protector, and that she would not tolerate my insistent demand that they rely solely on me. Perhaps it was simply a feeling inside her that I was going to have to earn my place with her again.

I didn't think of these things at the time but just followed an instinct to walk over to sit next to my oldest daughter. I even held my tongue, for once not scolding her, not mentioning the berries she'd used and managing to laugh at the purple faces around me.

"Here," I said, "taste one." I scooped a fat blackberry from my pail and popped it between Amanda's lips. She smiled as if it were her first berry, though we both knew she'd eaten plenty while she picked. As she chewed she looked at me, intently, in a way she hadn't since she'd been home. I looked back at her, past the veneer of purple, into what was too often a dead-serious, heavy-with-responsibility, young girl's face.

Mollie crawled over to sit in my lap and Mary stood up behind me, draping her arms over my shoulders and pressing her gooey cheek into my hair. Mary reached over me to pluck a few berries from the bucket; Mollie dipped in for a few, too. Stephanie got a handful. Amanda took some more. I set the pail aside on a flat piece of ground and before I could decide if I were willing to give up my fruit, the four girls dug in. They filled their mouths and spit tiny seeds and rubbed berries across their lips to make them even darker. Then Mary picked one out of the pail to punch into my mouth. Instead of chewing so it went down fast, I let the berry come apart on my tongue. I closed my eyes and tipped my head back a little so the afternoon sun could fall on my face. The berry tasted, I decided, the way that sunshine felt.

"Aren't they good?" Stephanie asked me, leaning against my arm and leaving a violet print on my skin.

"Yes," I said. "They're delicious."

On the way back down the hill, Mollie was again on my back, resting her cheek sleepily against my shoulder and smearing more juice on my clothes. The other three ran ahead, unleashed. I hiked my youngest up to a more comfortable spot, set my feet on the path so I wouldn't slip, and let myself believe that for at least this moment we were okay. At least for this day.

The girls turned a corner on the trail so I could no longer see them, but in a few seconds I heard Mary's voice drifting back. "Pis-gah!" she shouted, then again. Stephanie's voice, then Amanda's, joined in. "Pisgah! Pisgah!"

They'd seen the bird—or imagined they had. Far down the hill from me they'd found danger and lifted their masked faces to the sky to shout it away. They didn't need me to help them; in some deep way I couldn't bear to recognize, they knew how to take care of themselves. "Pisgah!" I heard again, more faintly. I hoisted Mollie up to the place on my hips where she fit perfectly, and I kept walking, the strain of the path sharp in my shins and thighs.

I longed to hurry and catch up with Stephanie and Mary, and with Amanda who surely led this small pack, but then I convinced myself to stay slow and steady on the trail. The thing I wanted most—for my daughters to be fully, instantly, mine—wasn't going to happen. It probably wasn't even a good idea, the volume of the yearning in my chest concerning their return. My children were different people now, altered by the need to adjust to two different houses and to parents who no longer created a united front. If their world was less safe, I'd helped make it so. Walk on—that was all I could do. Walk until I found my daughters at the end of the trail and, together, we all went home.

Barbara Kingsolver

Civil Disobedience at Breakfast

I have a child who was born with the gift of focus, inclined to excel at whatever she earnestly pursues. Soon after her second birthday she turned to the earnest pursuit of languor, and shot straight through the ranks to world-class dawdler. I thought it might be my death.

Like any working stiff of a mother keeping the family presentable and solvent, I lived in a flat-out rush. My daughter lived on Zen time. These doctrines cannot find peace under one roof. I tried everything I could think of to bring her onto my schedule: five-minute countdowns, patient explanations of our itinerary, frantic appeals, authoritarianism, the threat of taking her to preschool *exactly* however she was dressed when the clock hit seven. (She went in PJs, oh delight! Smug as Brer Rabbit in the briars.) The more I tried to hurry us along, the more meticulously unhurried her movements became.

My brother pointed out that this is how members of the Japanese Parliament carry out a filibuster—by shuffling up to the voting box so extremely slowly it can take one person an hour to get across the room, and a month or two to get the whole vote in. It's called "cow walking," he reported. Perfect, I said. At my house we are having a Cow Life.

And that's how it was, as I sat at breakfast one morning watching my darling idle dangerously with her breakfast. I took a spectacularly deep breath and said, in a voice I imagined was calm, "We need to be going very soon. Please be careful not to spill your orange juice."

She looked me in the eye and coolly knocked over her glass.

Bang, my command was dead. Socks, shirt, and overalls would have to be changed, setting back the start of my workday another thirty minutes. Thirty-five, if I wanted to show her who was boss by enforcing a five-minute time-out. She knew exactly what she was doing. A filibuster.

I'd been warned the day would dawn when my sweet, tractable daughter would become a Terrible Two. And still this entirely predictable thing broadsided me, because in the beginning she was *mine*—as much a part of my body, literally, as my own arms and legs. The milk I drank knit her bones in place, and her hiccups jarred me awake at night. Children come to us as a dramatic coup of the body's fine inner will, and the process of sorting out "self" from "other" is so gradual as to be invisible to a mother's naked soul. In our hearts, we can't expect one of our own limbs to stand up one day and announce its own agenda. It's too much like a Stephen King novel.

Later in the day I called a friend to tell my breakfast war story. She had a six-year-old, so I expected commiseration. The point of my call, really, was to hear that one could live through this and that it ended. Instead, my friend was quiet. "You know," she said finally, "Amanda never went through that. I worry about her. She works so hard to please everybody. I'm afraid she'll never know how to please herself."

A land mine exploded in the back of my conscience. My child was becoming all I'd ever wanted.

The way of a parent's love is a fool's progress, for sure. We lean and we lean on the cherished occupation of making ourselves obsolete. I applauded my child's first smile, and decoded her doubtful early noises to declare them "language." I touched the ground in awe of her first solo steps, as if she alone among primates had devised bipedal locomotion. Each of these events in its turn—more than triumph and less than miracle—was a lightening, feather by feather, of the cargo of anxious hope that was delivered to me with my baby at the slip of our beginning.

"We teach our children one thing only, as we were taught: to wake up," claims Annie Dillard. That's just about the whole truth, a parent's incantation. Wake up, keep breathing, look alive. It's only by forming separateness and volition that our children relieve us of the deepest parental dread: that they might somehow *not* wake up, after all, but fail to thrive and grow, remaining like Sleeping Beauty in the locked glass case of a wordless infancy. More times than I could count, in those early days, I was stopped in the grocery by some kindly matron who exclaimed over my burbling pastel lump of baby, "Don't you wish you could keep them like that forever?" Exactly that many times, I bit the urge to shout back, "Are you out of your mind?"

From the day she emerged open-mouthed in the world, I've answered my child's cries with my own gaping wonder, scrambling to part the curtains and show the way to wakefulness. I can think or feel no more irresistible impulse. In magnificent pantomime, I demonstrate to my small shadow the thousand and one ways to be a person, endowed with opinions. How could it be a surprise that after two years the lessons started to take? The shadow began to move of its own accord, exhibiting the skill of opinion by any means necessary. Barreling pell-mell through life was not my daughter's style; a mother ought to arrange mornings to allow time for communing with the oatmeal—that was her first opinion. How could I fail to celebrate this new red-letter day? There had been a time when I'd reduced my own personal code to a button on my blue-jeans jacket that advised: question authority. A few decades later, the motto of my youth blazed resplendent on my breakfast table, the color of Florida sunshine. I could mop up, now, with maternal pride, or eat crow.

Oh, how slight the difference between "independent" and "ornery." A man who creates spectacular sculptures out of old car bodies might be a wonderful character, until he moves in next door. Children who lip off to their parents are cute in movies because they're in movies, and not in our life. Another of my brother's wise nuggets, offered over the phone one Saturday while I tried to manage family chaos and pour a cement porch foundation, was: "Remember, kids are better in the abstract than in the concrete." Of all kid abstractions, independence may be the hardest one to accept in the concrete, because we're told how we'll feel about it long before it arrives. It's the mother of all childhood stereotypes, the Terrible Twos.

Now there are stereotypes that encircle a problem like a darn good corral, and there are stereotypes that deliver a problem roaring to our doorstep, and I'm suspicious of this one, the Terrible Twos. If we'd all heard half so much about, say, the "Fat Fours," I'd bet dollars to donuts most four-year-olds would gain lots of weight, and those who didn't would be watched for the first sign of puffiness. Children are adept at becoming what we expect them to be. "Terrible" does not seem, by any stretch, to be a wise expectation. My Spanish-speaking friends—who, incidentally, have the most reliably child-friendly households in my acquaintance—tell me there's no translation for "Terrible Twos" in their language.

The global truth, I think, is that the twos are time-consuming and tidiness-impaired, but not, intrinsically, terrible. A cow in parliament is not a terrible cow. It's just a question of how it fits in with the plan.

The plan in our culture, born under the sign of freedom with mixed-message ascendant, is anyone's guess. The two developmental stages we parents are most instructed to dread—the twos and teens—both involve a child's formation of a sovereign identity. This, a plumb horror of assertive children, in the land of assertiveness training and weekend seminars on getting what you want through creative visualization. Expert advice on the subject of children's freedom is a pawnshop of clashing platitudes: We are to cultivate carefully the fragile stem of self-esteem. We are to consider a thing called "tough love," which combines militarist affection with house arrest, as remedy for adolescent misbehavior. We are to remember our children are only passing through us like precious arrows launched from heaven, but in most states we're criminally liable for whatever target they whack. The only subject more loaded with contradictions is the related matter of sex, which—in the world we've packaged for adolescents—is everywhere, visibly, the goal, and nowhere allowed. Let them eat it, drink it, wear it on their jeans, but don't for heaven's sakes pass out condoms, they might be inspired to do it. This is our inheritance, the mixed pedigree of the Puritans and Free Enterprise. We're to dream of our children growing up to be decision makers and trend setters, and we're to dream it through our teeth, muttering that a trend-setting toddler is a pain, and a teenager's decisions are a tour down the River Styx. How, then, to see it through?

The traditional camp says to hold the reins hard until the day we finally drop them, wish our big babies Godspeed, and send them out to run the world. I say, Good luck, it sounds like we'll have men and women with the mental experience of toddlers running domestic and foreign policy. (And, in fact, it sometimes appears that we do.) This is the parenting faction that also favors spanking. Studies of corporal punishment show, reliably, that kids who are spanked are more likely to be aggressive with their peers. For all the world, you'd think they were just little people, learning what they were taught.

I hold with those who favor allowing kids some freedom to work out problems their own way, and even make some messes, before we set them on Capitol Hill. I do not hold that this is easy. The most assiduous task of parenting is to divine the difference between boundaries and bondage. In every case, bondage is quicker. Boundaries, however carefully explained, can be reinterpreted creatively time and again. Yes, it's okay to pet the dog, and yes again on taking a bath, but *not* the dog *in* the tub. No to painting on the wall, no again to painting on the dog. I spent many years sounding to myself like Dr. Seuss: Not in a box! Not with a fox! Not on a train! Not in the rain!

The hardest boundaries to uphold are those that I know, in my heart, I have drawn for no higher purpose than my own convenience. I swore when I was pregnant I would never say to my child those stupid words "Because I said so!" Lord, have mercy. No contract I've ever signed has cost me so much. "Because I said so!" is not a real reason. But how about "Because if you do that again Mommy will scream, run into the bushes, pluck out the ovaries that made you, and cast them at the wild dogs." What price mental health? When your kid knocks over the orange juice, or ditches school, do you really have to listen to her inner wishes or can you just read the riot act?

Maybe both. Maybe there's not time for both right this minute —there never is, because life with children always bursts to fullness in the narrowest passages, like a life raft inflating in the emergency exit. If that's the case, then maybe the riot act now, and the other, listening to inner wishes, as soon as possible after you've worked free of the burning wreck.

During my short tenure as a parent I've relived my own childhood in a thousand ways while trying to find my path. Many of the things my parents did for me—most, I would say—are the things I want to do for my own child. Praise incessantly. Hold high expectations. Laugh, sing out loud, celebrate without cease the good luck of getting set down here on a lively earth.

But the world has changed since *Howdy Doody Time*, and some things nearly all parents did back then have been reconsidered. Spanking is one. Another, a little harder to define, has to do with structuring the family's time. My mother's job was me. But now I'm a mother with other work too, and fewer hours each day to devote to my main preoccupation of motherhood. I represent the norm for my generation, the throng of maternal employed, going about the honest work of the planet with gusto and generally no real alternative. The popular wisdom is that families used to be more kid-centered than they are now. I'm not so sure that's true. It's just different. My mother had kids to contend with from dawn till doom. She was (is) educated, creative, and much of the time the only people around for her to talk with had snakes in their pockets. My father worked very hard, as good fathers verily did. I had the guarantee of three squares daily, the run of several hundred acres of farms and wild Kentucky hills, the right to make a pet of anything nonvenomous, and a captive audience for theatrical projects. When my mother is canonized, I will testify that she really did sit through a hundred virtually identical productions, staged by my siblings and me, of the play titled approximately "The Dutch Boy Who Saved His Town by Putting His Finger in the Hole in the Dike." I have no idea why we did this. It seems truly obsessive. I can only offer as defense that we had a soft gray blanket with a hole in it, an irresistible prop. We took rave reviews for granted.

We also understood clearly that, during major family outings and vacations, our parents needed desperately to enjoy themselves. They bundled us into the back of the station wagon and begged us to go into hibernation for two thousand miles, so they could finish a conversation they'd started the previous autumn. I'm sure there were still plenty of times they sacrificed their vacation goals on the altar of my selfishness; I have forgotten these entirely. What I particularly remember instead is one nonstop auto trip to Key West, during which my sibs and I became bored beyond human limits. "Try counting to a million," my father suggested. And this is the point I am getting to: we actually did.

This seems amazing to me now. I could claim to be a victim, but that would be fatuous; my childhood was blessed. In the spectrum of the completely normal fifties family, nuclear units kept pretty much to themselves, and in the interest of everyone's survival, kids had to learn a decent show of obedience.

I'm amazed by the memory of counting to one million in a station wagon, not because I resent having done it myself, but because I can't imagine asking my daughter to do that, or, more to the point, *needing* for her to do it. When she and I head out on a car trip, we fall right into a fierce contest of White Horse Zit or license-plate alphabet. Childish enterprises, since they aren't my job, are in a sense my time off, my vacation. In spite of the well-publicized difficulties of balancing career and family, when I compare my life to my mother's I sometimes feel like Princess Grace. Each day I spend hours in luxurious silence, doing the work I most love; I have friends and colleagues who talk to me about interesting things, and never carry concealed reptiles. At the end of the day, when Camille and I are reunited after our daily cares, I'm ready for joyful mayhem.

For this reason I was also prepared to search through the pockets of my own soul on the day she and I arrived at our orange-juice impasse. I kept up a good authoritarian front at the time but understood my daughter's implicit request. What was called for here was some Cow Time, stress free, no holds barred. I decided that after work we would go somewhere, out of the house, away from the call of things that require or provoke an orderly process. Together my two-year-old and I would waste the long last hours of an afternoon.

We went to the zoo. Not very far *into* the zoo, actually; we made it through the front gate and about twenty steps past, to the giant anteater den. There Camille became enraptured with the sturdy metal railing that was meant, I gather, to hold the public back from intimate contact with the giant anteaters. There was no danger, so I let her play on the metal bar.

And play.

After ten minutes I longed to pull her on toward the elephants, because frankly there's only so much looking a right-minded person can do at a giant anteater. But our agenda here was to have no agenda. I did my part. Looked again at those long anteating noses and those skinky anteating tongues.

Other children materialized on the bar. They clung and they dropped, they skinned the cat and impersonated tree sloths, until their parents eventually pulled them off toward the elephants. My eyes trailed wistfully after those departing families, but I knew I was being tested, and this time I knew I could win. I could refrain from asking my toddler to hurry up even longer than she could persist in sloth. After something less than an hour, she got down from the bar and asked to go home.

Five years have passed since then. Now it sometimes happens that Camille gets up, dresses herself in entirely color-coordinated clothes, and feeds the dog, all before the first peep of the alarm clock. I never cease to be amazed at this miracle, developmental biology. For any parent who needs to hear it today, I offer this: whatever it is, you can live through it, and it ends.

Plenty of psychologists have studied the effects of parents' behavior on the mental health of their children, but few have done the reverse. So Laurence Steinberg's study of 204 families with adolescents broke some new ground. All the families lived in Wisconsin but were otherwise diverse: rural, urban, white, black, brown, single-parented, remarried, nuclear. Steinberg uncovered a truth that crosses all lines: teenagers can make you crazy. Forty percent of the study parents showed a decline in psychological well-being during their children's adolescence. Steinberg even suggests that the so-called midlife crisis may be a response to living with teenagers, rather than to the onset of wrinkles and gray hair per se. The forty-five-year-old parent with a thirteen-year-old, it turns out, is far more disposed to crisis than the forty-year-old parent with an eight-year-old. Marital happiness tends to decline in households with teens, and single parents are more likely to experience difficulty with remarriage. But the study produced one hopeful note for the modern parent: in all family configurations, work is a buffer. Parents with satisfying careers had the best chance of sailing through the storm of their children's adolescence.

Here at last is a rallying cry for the throng of maternal employed. The best defense against a teenager's independence, and probably a toddler's as well, may simply be a matter of quitting before we're fired. Or not *quitting*, exactly, but backing off from eminent domain, happily and with dignity, by expressing ourselves in the serious pursuits and pleasures that we hold apart from parenting.

Individuation goes both ways: we may feel less driven to shape a child in our own image if instead we can shape policy or sheet metal, or teach school, or boss around an employee or two. Luckiest of all is the novelist: I get to invent people who will live or die on the page, do exactly what I wish, *because I said so!*

I'm told it is terribly hard to balance career and family and, particularly, creativity. And it is, in fact. Good mothering can't be done by the clock. There are days I ache to throw deadlines to the wind and go hunt snipes. I wish for time to explain the sensible reason for every "no." To wallow in "yes," give over to a cow's timetable, stop the clock, stop watching the pot so it might splendidly boil.

I also long for more time of my own, and silence. My jaw drops when I hear of the rituals some authors use to put themselves in the so-called mood to write: William Gass confesses to spending a couple of hours every morning photographing dilapidated corners of his city. Diane Ackerman begins each summer day "by choosing and arranging flowers for a Zenlike hour or so." She listens to music obsessively, then speed-walks for an hour, every single day. "I don't know whether this helps or not," she allows, in *A Natural History of the Senses*. "My muse is male, has the radiant, silvery complexion of the moon, and never speaks to me directly."

My muse wears a baseball cap, backward. The minute my daughter is on the school bus, he saunters up behind me with a bat slung over his shoulder and says oh so directly, "Okay, author lady, you've got six hours till that bus rolls back up the drive. You can sit down and write, *now*, or you can think about looking for a day job."

As a mother and a writer, I'd be sunk if either enterprise depended on corsages or magic. I start a good day by brushing my teeth; I don't know whether it helps or not, but it does fight plaque. I can relate at least to the utilitarian ritual of Colette, who began her day's writing after methodically picking fleas from her cat. The remarkable poet Lucille Clifton was asked, at a reading I attended, "Why are your poems always short?" Ms. Clifton replied, "I have six children, and a memory that can hold about twenty lines until the end of the day."

I would probably trade in my whole Great Books set for an epic-length poem from the pen of Lucille Clifton. But I couldn't wish away those six distracting children, even as a selfish reader, because I cherish Clifton's work precisely for its maternal passions and trenchant understanding of family. This is the fence we get to walk. I might envy the horses that prance unbridled across the pastures on either side of me, but I know if I stepped away from my fence into the field of "Only Work" or "Only Family," I would sink to my neck. I can hardly remember how I wrote before my child made a grown-up of me, nor can I think what sort of mother I would be if I didn't write. I hold with Dr. Steinberg: by working at something else I cherish, I can give my child room to be a chip off any old block she wants. She knows she isn't the whole of my world, and also that when I'm with her she's the designated center of my universe. On the day she walks away from my house for good, I'll cry and wave a hanky from my lonely balcony; then I'll walk to my study, jump for joy, and maybe do the best work of my life.

It's never easy to take the long view of things, especially in a society that conveys itself to us in four-second camera shots. But in a process as slow and complex as parenting, an eye to the future is an anchor. Raising children is a patient alchemy, which can turn applesauce into an athlete, ten thousand kissed bruises into one solid confidence, and maybe orneriness to independence. It all adds up. From the get-go I've been telling my child she is not just taking up space here, but truly valuable. If she's to believe it, I have to act as if I do. That means obedience is not an absolute value. Hurting people is out of the question, but an obsession with the anteater bar can and will be accommodated. I hope to hold this course as her obsessions grow more complex. For now, whenever the older, wiser parents warn, "Just wait till she's a teenager," I smile and say, "I'm looking forward to that." They think I am insane, impudent, or incredibly naïve. Probably I am. Call it creative visualization.

My time here is up today, for I'm being called to watch a theatrical production entitled approximately "The Princess Fairy Mermaids Who Save the Castle by Murderizing the Monsters and Then Making Them Come Back Alive with Fairy Dust and Be Nice." I've seen this show before. Some days I like it, especially when they tie up the monster with Day-Glo shoelaces and pantyhose. Other days my mind drifts off to that spare, uncluttered studio where I will arrange flowers, Zenlike, when I'm sixty. I'll write great things, and I'll know once and for all the difference between boundaries and bondage.

Marjorie Sandor

Solomon's Blanket

When my husband and I separated, there arose the problem of where to keep our daughter's beloved "sheep blankie," a blanket already small, already so worn that its stuffing was falling out and the sheep themselves had faded to white. I was the one wanting to leave our marriage and, as such, found myself performing the dark ritual of rupture, tearing, in ways small and large, the fabric we'd woven for twelve years, never checking the seams. I asked a friend to split the blanket in half for me and sew up the open ends. So now there were two sheep blankies where before there was one, each diminished, and their inevitable ruin charged with deeper significance.

"The Solomonic sheep blankie," said my husband, with a sober, warning look, when I handed him his half. He was right, of course, and I knew it. The spiritual cost of leaving was unknowable, and I was beginning to see that it would come out over the seasons, like the unpredictable winter weather of our Northwest valley, a landscape where, in this season, a squall rises up over the coastal mountains, runs its course, and subsides, only to be followed hard upon by the next. It is difficult, even in the best of times, to remember the greening of the valley that begins under the low and rolling tumult of clouds gathering force over the ocean, where we can't see it.

Our daughter herself is the baby of Solomon's challenge, in

that story in which two women vie for possession of a newborn and the King calls for a knife to divide the living child in two, "that they may each take a half." So it seems to me, anyway, when I hear Hannah tell her teachers and friends with stunning directness, "Did you know I'm separated?" There is nothing more true: she is divided between us, the separated halves of our influence, our selves carried in herself. She carried us inside her before this, I know, but then the two halves were mingled—who knew where one left off and the other began? Who ever thought about it? This is something we are usually granted to know about our parents long after we are grown, and they are gone.

But Hannah, at six, is doing the heavy work of conveying stories between our houses, carrying our identities themselves. The stories are always beautiful ones, romantic even, and in her voice is wistful pride and a hint of wise admonishment, for the moments of discovery and beauty we each miss by seeing her only half the time. At Daddy's, she tells me, there is a wild mouse. They have never actually seen her, she says, but this mouse—a girl mouse of course—is there as sure as anything. Hannah has even named her: Wild Blackberry, for this is what the mouse would eat, if she were given the choice. Conversely, I've heard her tell her father on the telephone about my new landlady's ancient cat, nineteen years old, playful and loud voiced, but with a diagnosis of liver damage. Hannah regularly says a prayer for this cat, whose name is Nesta. *Please don't let her die yet.* Nesta's very name calls up the single nest of the ideal childhood; the cat herself is a tough survivor whose death we can only hope will be delayed until it is less painful.

There are darker currents than this. They are harder to detect, more troubling, and I find myself praying that these too will pass like our valley storms, bringing glimpses of light between, and the slow greening beneath. But when she is in one of those moods, it is the very darkness itself. She recently drew a self-portrait of a girl in tears, out of whose mouth comes "ha ha," and arching over, where a year ago a rainbow would have been, are the words "I am nothing." To read this is to be scalded by grief and fear. Yet when I asked her what "nothing" felt like, she gave me the key to helping her: she pointed to a precise spot between her heart and stomach, and said, "I feel it here, when I think of you and Dad when you used to be together."

The place where we were once joined in her is a real land-scape between heart and gut—a place I am afraid to journey. And how to go there? What words would carry me inside of her and what could I bring there, what healing instrument do I have that is as powerful as a child's wish to go back to the unity she was promised, in the deepest way, by being born to us and brought this far between us? Her own load, our own hearts and guts gone heavy with anger and grief and confusion, she carries. What can I do but try to carry some of it for her; take some of it, offer a "lightening" as physically as I can? So on those nights when she is with me, and I am putting her to bed, I lay my hand on her small warm belly and rub in a circle. "Oh, Mom," she says. "That feels so good. Can you do that every night?"

The swirl of darkness and the desire for the return of unity—of light—will live in her forever now: there will be a mystery of where God went, so long ago, and our waiting for that return. The tug of us, that which created her then broke apart, will be a wish that lives in her like religious faith, her eyes forever trained on the secret story of the world. Maybe, just maybe, it will give her the faith to trust that no mortal's answer will ever be the right and only one.

Each of the blanket's halves is still intact, though she recently told me that the one at Daddy's house has lost most of its stuffing and is, as she put it, pretty wrecked. She looked at me long and hard. Could I come to the house and fix it? I held her hands and composed my answer carefully, knowing now the power of the word. "I can't, sweetie," I said. "I'm sorry." Someday soon, only she will know what that blanket once really looked like: the sole archaeologist of her own early life, studying the artifact of a lost country, or a mountain reshaped by rough weather.

She's been asking me, lately, if God made us, then who made God? Nobody knows, I say, and I tell her a story I heard once when I was young, a creation myth from the Zohar, the thirteenth-century book of Jewish mysticism.

One day, I tell her, God was feeling lonely, sort of empty inside, and he sighed his loneliness into a little space of nothing, and it exploded, like a great big sneeze. Thus was the universe created, a darkness full of burning lights and bits of rock, where life itself would begin, over and over. So it is that everything in the world has a spark of the Divine inside of it—trees, rocks, you name it, I say.

Even me? she asks. I have a spark inside me? Where is it?

What luck a story brings; how often do we get this chance? I put my hand on the place she has shown me, between heart and gut; the place that aches and remembers; that sometimes feels like nothing.

That's where it is, I tell her. Right there.

Gina Petrie

Kicking and Screaming
(but Going Anyway)

The cover of our wedding invitation shows a picture drawn by my stepdaughter Caroline (then five): Greg is smiling, intoxicated with happiness. With his toes pointed downward, he is just beginning to float. I am the largest in the picture by far, with giant lips and heart-shaped shoes. Caroline is in the middle, joyful and proud. The other three, Greg's daughter, Kaitrin, fifteen, his son, Peter, fourteen, and my son, Isaac, four, are standing behind and to the right, their arms around each other, smiling as if content.

The afternoon that Caroline drew the picture, Greg and I picked it up, put it down, picked it up again, unsure what it was in this image that fascinated us so. Somehow, there in the curves and lines, Caroline had captured what we were about—what we really felt about this thing we were trying to build and be a part of.

At our wedding reception, long after Kaitrin asked to change the music being played in the reception hall, after Peter disappeared in the crowd with his cousins, after Caroline cried about tearing her brand-new tights, and after Isaac took off his suspenders and gave them to Kaitrin, telling her to "give these to some little boy who needs them," a friend approached me.

"Your invitation...," he said. "I can't stop looking at it. It's the clearest picture of yearning I've ever seen."

111

Being a part of a stepfamily—choosing to *really* be here—is the greatest challenge I have yet taken on. Adjusting to stepfamily life is tough because the real crux of who I am is caught up in this struggle. Not the "who I am" that I like to present to the world, but the identity that I would rather sometimes forget. Surrounded by people who sometimes feel like strangers, I don't have the safety of clinging to my social selves—those parts of myself that always act in mature and rational ways, all the while remembering to use the right fork. The parts of me that show up in this place of stepfamily are sometimes ugly. And, yet, this place can be an arena for the most inexplicable kindnesses and forgiveness when I falter or stumble.

On a record-setting 106-degree day, the kids were tired and sweaty. We declared it "bath time" for Isaac and Caroline. They begged to take one together. Greg and I looked at each other and debated. (Will it keep them in there longer? Will they be able to handle the whole opposite sex thing?) We decided to take the chance. Greg cleaned up the dinner table while I ran the bath and got them into it. All the bath toys were still packed in boxes, so, in a moment of fun, I gave each of them a kitchen utensil to play with in the water. Shrieks of glee followed the mumblings of happy chatter until suddenly something went wrong. Both were crying. Greg and I entered the bathroom by different doors to find them standing in the bath, yelling, making no sense. We untangled it until we learned that they were fighting over the kitchen tools.

Thrashing her arms, Caroline yelled, "It's Gina's fault! She's the one who gave them to us!"

I felt my face grow ugly with anger. "Why you…!" I growled. I roughly grabbed the ladle from her, violently turned and rushed out. I trembled at the anger's strength.

Thrashing her arms, Caroline was really asking, *Is Gina just another big kid here? Will Daddy punish her just like he punishes us?*

Later, sweet-faced, in her pink nightgown, Caroline found me and apologized. We buried our faces near each other's, whispering.

Here is the deep dark truth: I am coming to grips with actually being a stepparent but just when I think I have accepted it, I realize that I'm still holding out, as if I can wiggle my way out of being a stepmom to three kids. That's what I did in labor with my son, as well. It really came to a point where I believed that if I just stared at some corner of the hospital room, if I just thought the right thought, the labor pains would go away. The process of birth would just stop. I could go home and about my business just as life had been before.

It's probably a defect in my personality: when the going gets tough, I silently wish it would all disappear. When all six of us are out and everything is calm and everyone under the voting age is relatively content for the moment, it's easy to be their stepmom. It's difficult when they are demanding or reticent to take responsibility. And, yet, I have to find a way to accept that I am their stepmom no matter what.

One Christmas while we were dating, we spent our first extended time all together at Greg's parents' house in Seattle. I sat with Nicole, Greg's sister-in-law, one afternoon when we heard the familiar sounds again in the living room: the cycle of Caroline misbehaving, being given a timeout, and then melting down. There had been a lot of screaming on Caroline's part during that vacation. The conversation at the table stopped, and I sat silent, waiting for the ruckus to end. It was at that point that Nicole did me a great kindness.

In a gentle voice she said, "You know…that isn't like Caroline. She's not really like this."

It took me off guard. Suddenly I realized that I had been so busy trying to tolerate Caroline's behavior that I hadn't a clue as to who Caroline really was. Of course, it was possible that she was more than a swirling bundle of actions and sounds that made me slightly uncomfortable; at that moment, I realized that maybe what I'd been seeing all that week, though real in its own way, was not really indicative of her identity. Who is Caroline? I asked myself, as I watched Greg lead her—heaving chest, red cheeks— off into another room. If not this screaming little person in front of me, who then?

That night she dazzled us all by singing a show tune complete with dancing. I held on to the vision of her remembering all the words as if tightly held in my fist, bound and determined to create a new vision of Caroline for myself, a vision of that charming smile as she danced.

Watching each other struggle with these questions of identity can be painful. There is a special sadness watching my son strain to figure out who this man is and what type of relationship he wants to have with him, and at times hurting Greg's feelings. Isaac will race toward Greg for a hug and then, somehow, his fists make an appearance. A classic "approach/avoidance" reaction, Greg says.

In his four-year-old way, he works through the issue, planning a trap (his latest interest since seeing the movie *Home Alone*) to catch Greg when he comes home from work. All day Isaac worked on the grand scheme, tying string across the front porch banisters, experimenting with different plastic insects to tie in the trap. At one point, Isaac came to find me.

He said, "Mom, I don't know how to make my trap."

"Honey, you've been working on it all day. It looks fine to me."

He paused for a moment and then said, "But I don't know what to do with the bugs. I could make them come out and hit Greg. I kind of want them to hit him…(then, in a small voice)… but, I also don't want them to hit him."

It is a relief to both of us when these words bubble up to the surface.

When Greg and I were engaged, one of my university students noticed the sudden appearance of a ring on my left hand. After class she congratulated me and shyly asked about my husband-to-be. As she walked with me to my office, I told her about Greg and his kids.

Kali said, "Oh, you'll be a stepmom! I grew up in a stepfamily, and I loved it."

Nearing my office door, I said, "So, give me some advice. What should a good stepmom do?"

"Just love them," she said with a surprising earnestness. "Just love those kids."

At the time, I wrote off Kali's response as good-hearted but naïve. All the books I was plowing through about stepfamilies were loaded with tips and strategies and warnings about dysfunctional pitfalls. It was far more complicated, certainly. Yet, now I know that Kali was right. If a stepmom-to-be approached me now and asked for advice, I would tell her what Kali told me. In every interaction with the kids—every cleanup of spilled milk, every dispute over which channel to watch, every struggle over a missed bus—I am faced with a choice: to act with love or to act without it. It is that simple. And that often means gritting my teeth and holding on to my own vision of who the kids are to me and who I want to be to them.

Once upon a time when I was young and majoring in chemistry, I believed in an objective truth, a truth discernible by those asking the right questions and looking in the right places. Now, much older, I have learned from my stepparenting that I choose what I want to see, what I want to focus on, and I draw conclusions based on these choices. More important than what is objectively true is what I want to happen and where I want to go.

I very much want to love these kids. So, I actively choose my vision of them. One challenging morning when I had a meeting to make, Caroline did not put on her coat or mittens or scarf or hat or shoes or backpack as I asked, and each of these tasks represented a battle and sharp words and then tears on Caroline's part. When we finally pulled up in front of school, Caroline and Isaac bounded out of the car but then Caroline ran back with her lips scrunched up into a pucker for one last kiss: one last kiss before the school day begins. That is the snapshot I keep from that day. Not the scenes in the foyer. The image of Caroline with lips puckered in that amazing way, waiting for her kiss. From me.

Back in the beginning, Peter and Kaitrin went through a

period of often physically placing themselves between Greg and me. If Greg and I were sitting on the couch and there was any room between us, Kaitrin would sit down in that space. Sitting down at the dinner table, before I even realized that I was expecting Greg to sit in the empty seat beside me, Peter instead would slip into the waiting chair.

Greg and I talked about the phenomenon a bit and wondered at the kids' motives. Although I feared that perhaps they liked me so little they were anxious for every opportunity to get between me and their dad, I realized that fear such as this would leave me feeling uncomfortable around the kids and looking for ways to withdraw. I realized that what I needed was to get closer to them. I lit a candle of hope and decided that they must like me—a lot. They must like me enough that they were looking for opportunities to be near me. This took me to a place of tenderness toward the kids.

I use Kali's words like a litmus test now; I choose the vision that brings about my acting towards the kids with love. I do this because that is who I want to be to the kids: someone who loves them.

In an intact, biological family, people take sides. Sometimes lines are drawn in the sand. But, ultimately, come nightfall, the members know that they all belong, that despite any cries of unfairness they are really all in the same boat. In a stepfamily, the fault line is already there. With a fleeting comment, we can set up our battle lines, toy soldiers ready to fight. His side; her side.

One Sunday, a tough moment occurred between Greg and me in the kitchen. Although it's a small room, all six of us happened to be in there. Silently, by a secret gesture, in a flash as if they had been practicing some covert maneuver, the children lined up. His against mine. His against me; mine against him.

It's the elephant in the living room. No matter what we do, I sometimes sulk to myself in my darker moments, we will always essentially be divided in two. But, despite my tendency to see the negative, despite the odds, slowly I witness us regrouping. Kaitrin teases her father at the table about one of his habits, and, agreeing, I gang up on him with her. A moment of shock flits across his face as he sees Kaitrin and me, together, gleeful in our teasing.

On another night at dinner, Isaac needed some help, and Peter rose to the task. "For a brother," said Peter, using some elbow-arm gesture I hazily recognized from pop culture. I took in his words and realized for the first time that Isaac did indeed have a brother. We six went out for ice cream, and while Greg stood among the crowd, waiting to order, I chatted with another mother. As she talked, I heard in her chatter that she assumed Kaitrin and Peter were Greg's kids; Caroline and Isaac were mine. I didn't correct her; I could feel myself smiling. These may be little signs, but I cling to them with hope.

As Greg and I work to make a home for all of us, I sometimes worry that I myself may never feel like home to my stepkids. Coming from a different gene pool, I know that my noises and phrases and idiosyncrasies are different than those to which Kaitrin, Peter, and Caroline are accustomed. Consequently, I grow anxious at the idea that although my stepkids may feel comfortable and safe and cared for at our home, they will never find their shoulders suddenly relaxing as they walk through the door or their breathing slowing down to a familiar pattern as they cross the threshold. I fret at the thought that though their father will always feel like home to them, the tidbits of me around the house will continue to be foreign to them, as if they are visiting someone else's house.

After Greg and I married, we took the kids back to my parents' farm in Indiana for a few days. I was proud to show this family off to the people I was from, and I proudly showed my husband and stepkids the place where I was raised. Days after the delightful trip, after everyone had returned to their daily rituals of school and work, Kaitrin told me that my parents' house felt like home to her. It was such a little comment, tucked inside another conversation, but it set off fireworks inside me. I could barely contain my glee. My parents' house felt familiar to Kaitrin, I decided, because I was beginning to feel familiar to her. I was no longer merely a foreign body in her world.

One afternoon, Isaac got frustrated and hit Caroline with a towel. A few moments of howling, accusations, yelling. Then they fled inside to me for justice, comfort, and assistance. We sorted it out. They apologized. They went back to the porch and I overheard the following:

> ISAAC: Will you still play with me?
> CAROLINE: Yes.
> ISAAC: Will you still love me?
> CAROLINE: Of course. I'm your sister, Ikey!
> ISAAC: Will you still be my sister?
> CAROLINE: You don't get it, do you? I'll always be your
> sister. Whether I want to be or not, I'm always going to be
> your sister.

Caroline got it right. Kicking or screaming, my family just keeps showing up anyway. That is our gift to each other. Unlike at the weddings of first-time brides and grooms, the presents stacked high at our wedding are not woks and toasters. What threatens to collapse the gift table is patience and determination.

Can the fissure ever be filled in and the two pieces brought together as if one? I can think of many reasons why it may not happen. Yet, after great loss for each of us in our first families, we are yearning, and a hesitant question arises: Will it ever be all right again?

The hesitancy comes because each of us cares so much about the answer, about what it means for our lives.

This past summer, Isaac, Caroline, and I went to pick up Kaitrin from a nearby cathedral where the camp bus was supposed to drop her. This part of parenting was new to me and not wanting to be late, we left early.

As we wandered around the grounds of the cathedral, the kids were excited to come upon an interesting pattern painted in the grass. Every summer, the folks at the cathedral create a labyrinth, a maze used for centuries as a means to inspire contemplation, to symbolize each individual's spiritual journey. Those found at Notre Dame de Chartres in France and Grace Cathedral in San Francisco are best known.

Caroline and Isaac were curious about what it was for and how it worked. I explained that walking along the path was a way to be quiet inside ourselves and to hear our own thoughts about our lives and our relationship to God. I also shared with them that each person who walks a labyrinth has thoughts about God— maybe even a name for God—unlike any other person's. Or maybe they are not thinking of God at all. The kids had shrugged off such ideas as these as pure chaos in past conversations: How could there be more than one idea of who God is? This time, however, their heads nodded and their eyes were wide.

"Let's walk it together!" they shouted in unison.

And so we did. Caroline entered first, then Isaac, and finally me. We followed the winding path, one just a few feet behind the other. Caroline walked with her hands held stiffly in prayer, her lips moving; Isaac skipped along, talking to himself every once in awhile; I felt myself relax, taking pleasure in the simple task of staying between the lines, my footfalls lulling me into my own prayerful thoughts. Despite our differences, we moved as if one. The kids' faces showed quiet pleasure and surprise when we all ended in the same place together. It felt like a miracle to me, too.

Nadine Chapman

The Demon's Looking Glass

I have been coming to this wooden chapel that looks like something transplanted from the Carpathian Mountains, gold dome and all, since Thanksgiving. I come because I sense something is wrong with one of my children. The senses, miserly sisters, only reveal so much. Whether they share forebodings or the occasional jolt of disquiet, the details are handled with parsimony. I do not know which child, older or younger, male or female, is the target of this new threat. So I fear for them all and pray in communion with the saints peering at me from each wall.

I think it is the icons that draw me here. They are paintings of real events and people, yet symbols at the same time. Through them I can step into the mystery of God's presence in the world, a mystery becoming denser for me each day. The reds of divinity layered with the blues and greens of humanity speak to this impossible journey called life in ways more difficult for my Roman Catholic tradition of strict logic, structure, and hierarchy to express. The icons are my companions. Here I rest among friends that honor a mother's inexpressible fear.

I learn the Eastern Rite Liturgy of Saint John Chrysostom from the fourth century. It seems like one long chanted conversation among priest, God, and congregation. No chance to drift off, to become paralyzed by ruminations about how little I may know, despite my best efforts, of the four children God has given me to nurture. Though I have nothing to go on but a feeling, it haunts me. And physical distance does not lessen that visceral tie linking me to each child; whether he or she is visiting a friend, away at camp, or trying out college for the first time makes no difference. The cry a mother wakes to before the sound fills her infant's mouth still calls to me from each of their developing bodies and minds, even in the early trial wanderings away from home. Gabriela Mistral says,

> But don't think he'll only be woven
> with my soul while I keep watch over
> him. When he wanders freely out in the
> streets, even though far away, the wind
> that lashes at him will tear my flesh and
> his cry will also rise in my throat....
> *(translated by Christiane Jacox Kyle)*

There is no escaping this full-bodied love the poet names in "Eternal Pain." Perhaps that is why the physical reality of my fear seeks these concrete images of spirituality found in this Byzantine Catholic Church: the richly textured priestly garments, whose every thread represents some nun's labor, the ever-present incense seeping into wood-paneled walls like ancient memory, the gold-leafed icon as a window to God.

Today, on the feast of St. Nicholas of Myra, my ability to move from one act to another depends on all that and much more. Today I see faith go out of my child's eyes.

It is only the beginning of revelations. When my daughter first tries to tell me, she cannot speak. Tears come like some great wave that never recedes. The man obsessed with her is a trusted instructor, a family man, a community icon. I won't know for some time about her experience with that insidious process called grooming—how the light touch on the arm to emphasize a point is sustained over time, how the brief pat of encouragement on the shoulder becomes the too-friendly hug. The stealthy dance of lust decked out in intimacy's white tuxedo feels cool and benign at first.

At sixteen she plays in her Catholic high school orchestra. She has studied three instruments—piano, viola, harp—and wants to try another one. Talent isn't her birthright, but she sees the musical scores in her head and practices. I go to sleep night after night to the strains of Pachelbel's Canon in D Major and strangely never tire of it. Playing with a small group and for competitions also helps in her struggle with inherent shyness. The search for a teacher starts. After gathering recommendations, we find a well-known college instructor and performer. My daughter learns quickly. She learns to trust this talented man. She labors for the perfect tone. There are music festivals, church solos, and concerts. My daughter and I attend some of her teacher's concerts together. His students get a special price so they can watch him onstage. So they can dream of their own debut. But this is no grunge rock star, no iconoclast Madonna. He's a man of the classics. By his own words, he spreads culture in the world. His tuxedo is always pressed, his coifed hair halo-like under the lights. He speaks with an urbane tone, an enlightened nonchalance.

Then comes the chance for a music scholarship. He helps her make an audition tape. His letter is crucial; he teaches at the college she will attend.

I have only fragments, but even these prove unbearable.

My daughter hands her father a letter her music instructor has written; she sits between us and weeps. We, her parents, shouldn't be too hard on her, the letter says. He has taught my daughter for three years, but assures us that for the first year and a half they were "just friends," sharing interests in poetry, animals, nature, and music. There is even a paragraph on his great concern for the environment, how his father always taught him to leave the world a cleaner place than he found it. For the last year, though, his life has been hard. He details the trials—caring for one sick relative night and day by choice and at great personal sacrifice, the need to visit another relative before it is too late. He offers graphic descriptions of the physical ravages he observes and his heroic responses. Despite his many obligations, he keeps giving. In the midst of all this, he discovers a special closeness with our daughter. Other responsibilities have kept him from dealing with the results of their mutual attraction, and he regrets these issues will have to wait again for one more emergency trip. He didn't intend for all things to become public yet, but now that others have become aware ... Somehow he will make possible our daughter's plans to become a physician and continue studying Greek ... or whatever. He never says how.

I cannot fathom this roué's long obsession with my child being detailed on the same page as an argument for recycling. Or that we should be relieved when he assures us he has worked through the age thing with her, gotten rid of the teenage boy who tried to date her.

Somehow his own wife and child never come up on his needy list. Neither do my daughter's siblings.

Afterward, the altar girl, the teenager who like St. Francis communes with the birds, will tell me how much she prayed but without ever getting an answer. A strange film clouds her vision, blocking out all light. Have her eyes been pierced by shards of the cruel demon's enchanted mirror that makes the good look ugly, the evil attractive? The demon's looking glass, masterpiece of distortion, circles the world in pieces until one lodges in a person's eye, making him or her abandon goodness. Will my daughter, like little Kai in the covetous tale of *The Snow Queen*, forget how to smile? Will her aborted youth leave her soul in a frozen void? She too has gazed into the glittering almond eyes of the seducer. The cruel spell cast on her by the kiss of one who promised warmth and self-mastery instead has chilled her heart. But like Kai, trapped in his seducer's icy maze of rooms and corridors, she no longer feels the cold. She feels nothing.

My heart is riven, split apart by a sledgehammer of deceit more brutal than anything I have ever known. Now I understand why church bells torture some ears. Why betrayal numbs the soul with its steady drip of pain that promises to go on forever. In the next moment, I am reduced to sentimentality: visions of pigtails, freckles, the childhood drawings of bold yellow suns and smiling faces. I see my daughter running across a hay field. A galloping pony, she stops to whinny, stops and turns over a rock by the creek to check for new life. Larvae of anything will do. Every life form requires attention. Every life form has its own trajectory, and she is determined to follow its arc.

I am left with either blankness or a maelstrom of jarring images. Nothing in between.

It hasn't occurred to me that this violence is hardly rare. But it's older than the Epic of Gilgamesh, a tale from the wisdom-tradition recited for almost three thousand years before the advent of Christianity. Gilgamesh, the unruly hero-king of Uruk, is a leader, bold and powerful. He sees into hidden places, knows secret things. Compared to a wild bull by his narrator, he tolerates no rivals. Though arrogance and passionate strength are part of his legendary aura, they cause problems. Parents wonder what they can do to save their virgin daughters from the lust-driven hero, for he "does not leave a girl to her mother." Men of the city complain that no daughter of a warrior or bride is safe from this "shepherd of the city" either.

Such stories only serve to elevate his superhuman allure. Still I hear the wistful discordant mutterings, always behind the scenes, always secondary to the main plot. Only Enkidu, another male of exceptional beauty and strength created by the gods to distract Gilgamesh's appetites, can affect his actions. Only someone like himself counts. Narcissism reigns. But when his close friend dies, Gilgamesh mourns for the first time; in this existential grief self-glory proves hollow. No woman or girl ever matters like that; no female rivets his imagination or triggers a spiritual quest.

But what of the daughters he could not leave to their mothers? Who will write the tale of their heroic spiritual battles? Who will grieve for their losses, these child women left to molder in the shadows, mere distractions on the hero's path? Even after the hero ravages them, it will be their duty to lay laurels at his feet and sing his praises. All for the good of the city, the culture, the state.

Two weeks after the letter, I am sitting at a tea table with the man who has treated my daughter's faith and trust like a playground for cynics. I have come at his request, but still he has to fit me in between appointments, meetings with a concert board.

I don't think you realize what a respected family I come from, he says. My father was a talented professional, my mother always involved—in civic and charitable organizations. And I brought culture to this community, he says. I've made a lasting contribution.

It is clear he is special. Anything like the regular rules of society don't apply here. Have they ever? I say I want him to leave my daughter alone. I plead with him to let her go, to let her develop and grow. He responds by detailing my daughter's inadequacies. She doesn't even know how to cook. It's some version of "I've had to teach her everything she knows." She needs his help to deal with her social ineptness, her lack of confidence, to bring her to his level. I can only pray she never makes it that far, that by some miracle she can escape such grandeur. That wild hope allows me to listen while this man treats my daughter's identity, her very being, like some concoction for a desert plate. I lift the tea cup from its saucer and let the hot liquid rage against my lip.

I am fighting for time—time for her to escape before he can stunt all vestiges of true independence. I tell him nothing justifies violating the teacher–student relationship, nothing justifies committing this crime against her, against everything it means to teach. There are handbooks, rules. He isn't worried. He may have to write a few letters. That's all. He is sure my daughter will do whatever he wants. And he lets me know what a lioness his wife is when it comes to any publicity that might hurt their child.

He is leveling the warning, ratcheting up the risk to my daughter for any action I take. My family's frantic calls to police, school officials, priests, and lawyers have already been made, but he believes he can mitigate everything. What is my daughter's value compared to his commercial worth, his connections? The cold calculation of it all hits me. When I suggest he find a therapist to help him understand the needs of inexperienced teenage girls, he doesn't see the relevance. After all, I could learn from the way he is raising his own child.

It is the first Sunday of December. This small Byzantine Catholic Church is celebrating the visit of St. Nicholas with a gift from the priest for every child, every adult. Snow softens the rigid earth as the congregation travels from the parish to a rented hall. The children, forced to put food before presents, race around tables to cope with the waiting. But it is not just the young who relish this ritual of giving; anticipation also radiates from the oldest faces. The most famous story about St. Nicholas, this fourth-century Bishop of Myra, tells of a poor nobleman who had three daughters. Because he could not raise the money for dowries, the young sisters could not marry and, therefore, faced a life of shame and degradation, even prostitution. Seeking a way to help the girls anonymously, Bishop Nicholas tosses three bags of gold through an open window in the house. Though it is night, the grateful father sees him.

My daughter keeps her arms crossed tight across her swollen belly and no one in the hall suspects. I can think of nothing else. "Do you understand what this means," I say more than ask, sure she is not grasping the extent of the calamity. As if I can.

It will be fine, she says.

How?

I've got it worked out.

How?

Mr. Bryce has to leave to see a sick relative, but that's just for a week or so. You don't have to worry. I don't want you to worry.

Her mouth is a stretched frozen line, but her forehead wrinkles. I'm asking too many questions. It hits me then that she has never called the father of the child developing inside her by his first name. He was Mr. Bryce at her first music lesson, and he is Mr. Bryce today. The look in my child's eyes matches nothing she says. Fear quivers just beneath the cockiness. I am overwhelmed with revulsion by what this teacher has done. How I wish the brilliance of her hair and eyes did not draw such attention. If only they had faded to dull anonymity before he ever saw her. What a blessing if some grotesque scar had marred the delicate skin. I am ashamed, but right now anything seems worth saving her from this bondage. At the same time, I know it's more than surface beauty that attracts. It's the admiring gaze, the unguarded adoration of youth mixed with vulnerability that the prestige-craving hero takes as rightful bounty for his conquests.

My daughter takes her gift from St. Nicholas, just as much in need of the patron of unmarried girls, the protector of virgins, as the daughters of almost sixteen centuries ago. The miracle seems more and more in just giving a young woman the chance to escape a craven hero's exploits, his lascivious gaze and call to be worshipped, while society blinks.

As a young mother, I spent much of my time chasing toddlers through the world. It is a literal, quite comforting act. How many times is a child snatched from possible danger in the form of a street, a steep staircase, a race down the aisle into strangers? But the day comes when there is no chance to intervene. The car accelerates and the child, just out of reach, lies twisted on black pavement. There is no discernible warning or the parent fails to recognize the signs. Danger has a shifting face; it likes to mask its identity and bury clues. There's always one more unlatched gate.

It is my child, more than anyone else I have known, who forces me to stop everything and wait for God. Her agony and confusion, the bravado of her effort to somehow satisfy the demands of her abuser, bear witness to that need. She repeats the magnanimity of his deeds just as he has related them. She believes he can get whatever he wants. And I know beneath all the effort she makes to excuse this man's self-righteous vanity, she is afraid. In "Spiritual Autobiography," Simone Weil explains that she never "sought for God." The expression strikes Weil as false. Neither does she pray, and yet God finds her, sitting in the twelfth-century chapel of Santa Maria degli Angeli during a tourist visit to Assisi. While she recites metaphysical poet George Herbert's "Love" poem, she feels the presence of God, something she had never considered possible before that moment. Because God comes to her without any effort on her part, she believes waiting for God on other issues is the only path to take. And wait she does, for the rest of her life, without succumbing to institutional pressures or escaping her own intense sufferings. This is never a passive journey.

It is not easy to watch my child's once faith-sparked eyes fade, as the grand manipulator, the pied piper of ego and desire, who cares nothing for the impact of his hero dalliance, replaces such faith with a mere reflection of his undisputed glory. Now the sole function of her life is to mirror his radiance. I have to accept that he will never understand what a graveyard he has dug for this developing woman and everyone who loves her. As a parent, I must wait for that moment when love's surplus of meaning spills out over this wasted desert landscape.

This is the day of gifts, no matter how incongruent that seems. This day anticipates the coming of the Christ child, the great anti-hero whose life lets me know the end of my daughter's story, even the story of daughters of the world, has not been told. There will be new interpretations that consider what Weil calls the act of *creative attention*, the ability to move from a force-based social rendering to the individual sufferer of social affliction. It is the story of one living not to extend power and prestige but of one who nurtures the life of those standing apart. Through love and justice, *creative attention* perceives what is invisible to the world of force, the individual sufferer. *Creative attention* abhors reducing another person to the mere reflection of someone else's glory. It fights to name what society does not see, and, therefore, says does not exist.

This vision requires exquisite movement toward a tragedy the social order chooses not to embrace. Society specializes in veneers—a few thousand years of layering over the existence of those who have no value are nothing. How quickly glossy language obfuscates brute force; institutions choose the narrowest interpretations of rules to tiptoe around the savaging of human dignity. All this so the idols of false hero worship can remain. How invested the world is in this meandering tale. Later I find out my daughter's abuser tells her he can't stand the college practice rooms. They have shoddy construction, aren't soundproof—the complaints go on and on. So he moves her music lessons to the park. He never fears investigation.

Creative attention seeks the restoration of grace by reaching out to the nameless afflicted and giving them a sacramental name. It requires the most focused union of intellect and spirit. On the feast of St. Nicholas, wonder worker, fourth-century giver of dowries to young women with no chance of achieving social protection, I see how vulnerable the modern age child remains: my daughter is one more emerging woman stacked against what Weil calls the psychological force "that does *not* kill, i.e., that does not kill just yet." When the soul is forced to live inside the body others treat as a thing, no part of that person's nature escapes the violence done to it. The burden is extraordinary. The result: a torquing of the soul.

But the child's name spoken with a parent's love *is* sacramental. All the powers of society directed to subsume individual affliction to the ravenous hero's needs must find this stumbling block. I do not know when or how the ice spell will be broken, or what it will take to wash demon glass out of my daughter's eyes. I do know about the force of love, like that in the unitive intellect and hand of Kai's sister, Gerda, as she reaches out to help her brother find again the pattern of love despite his seduced and unresponsive state. But she cannot succeed alone against the evil-hearted Snow Queen. Despite the treachery and obstacles Gerda must encounter on her journey, others offer aid.

I no longer see faith in my daughter's eyes, but she sits here beside me on this hard wooden bench among icons. Together we will leave the church and walk across the snow-covered landscape.

Nancy Mairs

Room for One More

One Saturday morning several years ago, when my mother and I were talking on the telephone as we do every week, she expressed regret at living on the other side of the country from my sister's girls. At that time my foster son, Ron, had returned with his family to Iceland for a second tour of duty, and so I commiserated with Mother. In our highly mobile society, grandmothering is apt to take place in crude, stop-motion: the lisping toddler in droopy diapers who gives you a milky kiss as he leaves your front door shows up at it next as a blur in blue jeans with the pockets full of marbles, his lips sticky under a red Kool-Aid moustache, and then maybe as a skate punk in RayBans and neon-bright jams, even his hair defying gravity....

"Oh," Mother said when I referred wistfully to Ron's boys, Alex and C.J., "but those aren't your *real* grandchildren." I wasn't so sure about that. They'd seemed real enough to me on their last visit to Cactus Grandma and Cactus Grandpa, as they call us, their solid sweaty little-boy bodies electric with energy. But of course the reality Mother was calling into question had to do not with their substance, which she had seen for herself, but with their entitlement to a particular claim upon me (and thus, at another remove, upon herself). Her point was that the boys and I shared no genetic material. Being related "by blood," this sharing is called, though since every cell has DNA one might just as well say "by snot," which would go a long way toward demystifying an essentially troublesome distinction.

"Blood is thicker than water," the adage goes, reflecting the primacy traditionally accorded to familial bonds by basing them not on mere proximity, an assortment of bodies gathered under one roof, but on consanguinity, the blood flowing through those bodies held in common. In these terms, I am connected to my own children more closely than I am not only to Ron and his sons but also to my children's father. The children and I don't literally share our blood, of course. During the brief period when we did, thanks to the presence of a factor in the their blood which is absent in mine, we proved so incompatible that now a transfusion of anybody's blood but my own could cause mine to "clump," a sort of blood-is-thicker-than-blood condition that I'm told would be very bad for me indeed. So we keep our precious bodily fluids to ourselves. All the same, I do feel connections with them I don't feel with anyone else, the essence of which I can't firmly identify.

I conceived Anne on Christmas Eve 1964, as I did just about everything else when I was twenty-one, because I was supposed to. I had been married a decent interval, which for Catholics might be nine months to the day from the wedding night but for Protestants was a little longer so as to demonstrate our enlightened use of birth control, and now a baby was expected of me. I wasn't at all reluctant, mind you, since my fulfillment depended on this step. In the same way that no woman who could find a husband would choose to remain a "spinster," no woman who could get pregnant would choose to remain childless. A woman who couldn't get pregnant could always adopt an infant (Catholic infants for Catholics and Protestant ones for Protestants, so that a blue-eyed, straw-haired family like mine didn't wind up with a baby whose wide black gaze and dark ringlets marked her outsider status), but adoption was second-best and the woman who had to settle for it was not only pitied but ever-so-slightly scorned because she "couldn't have" children. (Since her husband's sperm count was never mentioned, the deficiency was at least tacitly ascribed to her.) So I was relieved when my pregnancy was confirmed. Marriage had let me down a bit, but this time I was definitely on my way to fulfillment.

The funny thing is that I really was on my way, but the route was so circuitous and fulfillment so different from anything I'd been led to expect that I spent years in a panic, certain I'd taken one wrong turn after another, certain I was irredeemably lost in the Black Bog of Bad Motherhood. I suspect now that other women were stumbling and sloshing through the same terrain, but the Bog's distinctive feature is a miasma so thick that nothing—not a footfall, not a groan or whimper—penetrates it. One is only alone there. As far as I could tell, every other woman was managing motherhood as though she were born to it; and so closely did I control my terror and chagrin most of the time that every other woman may have thought that I was doing the same.

Anne was born, and remained, a golden girl: smart, funny, self-possessed, the kind who talks whole sentences at a year and learns to read in nursery school and sails straight on to become a National Merit Scholar, graduate from Smith *magna cum laude*, join the Peace Corps, enter graduate school, marry the man you'd have chosen if arranged marriages were still in vogue…. At about the time she was exiting her teens, I asked her how come she'd never rebelled, and she shrugged: "I guess I never saw any need to." True enough. From birth, she'd done as she damned well pleased; luckily for her, what pleased her to do pleased the rest of us as well. Even a child this easy proved too much for me, however, and when she was two I turned her over to my mother for the six months I spent in a mental hospital. Although the reasons for my breakdown were complicated, as I've suggested here and elsewhere, at the time I perceived them to coalesce around my inability to take care of—or even to "want"—my own child.

Nonetheless, pressured again by social expectations and also by George, himself an only child, I was determined to have another baby. But because of our Rh incompatibility, Matthew was born jaundiced. Snatched from my vagina, given an exchange of blood, and deposited in an isolette, he was a week old before I was allowed to touch him, and whatever bonding might have taken place at birth was aborted. We have spent the rest of our lives trying to recover from this trauma. Once, when I asked an elderly friend if she regretted not having children, she responded in her characteristically forthright manner: "It was the great tragedy of my life." Each life must hold one, I think: one pain that overarches and obscures all others, one haunting irreversible fault for which one can never atone. Matthew's botched birth constitutes my great tragedy.

From the outset he cried through most of his waking hours, all the more fiercely if I held and cuddled him; grief-stricken at his rejection, I retreated into the role of caretaker, dutiful enough but distant and wary. For years, I believed that I didn't love him: "He was the most heart-breakingly beautiful baby I've ever seen," I reflected in my journal, "and I rejected him wholly…. This must be the bitterest thing that can happen to a woman, to be deprived of her own child in this way—worse than death, because then one can go on loving the lost child—a kind of death in life, to have the child but not the love." I felt certain that he knew of my failure and despised me for it: "I'm so ashamed in the face of his knowledge that I can hardly bear to be with him. I wonder if there'll ever come a time when he can understand my grief, forgive me even. No, why should he?"

As he entered the tumultuous and defiant adolescence Anne had never seen a need for, I could scarcely stand the sight of him, "both sides of his head shaved, the hair on top sticking up in clumps. Neck and arms draped with chains and padlocks, studded strips of leather, filthy camouflage bandannas, loud neckties. His clothing from Value Village (cheap, at least), ill fitting, the colors clashing." According to the "imaginary-ideal-Matthew" theory his father and his grandparents subscribed to, "inside this hideous exterior is a heart of gold, a fine upstanding young man, a brilliant student, impeccably dressed and aesthetically refined, if only one could find the key to set him free. I don't subscribe. There's only one Matthew. What you see is what you get. So let him be."

Only gradually did it occur to me that these complicated responses—grief at the other's rejection, terror for the other's well-being and guilt for endangering it, attention to the minutest aspects of the other's condition, defense of the other's right to choose his own way—are the marks not of repulsion but of passionate attachment. Everything in my experience and education had suggested that "love" was reactive, an upwelling of delight caused by the beloved's pleasing looks or ways. My beloved did not please me. In fact, much of the time he drove me stark ravers. But he absorbed me utterly. And still does. Just this morning we were playing computers, a sport that highlights not only the quickness and grace of his mind but also his tact as a teacher. I'm installing a new system and turning my old one over to him, a process that would render me paralytic with stupidity if he didn't keep reassuring me that what we're having here is *fun*. Now he's gone off, and my studio, which generally looks as though a whirlwind had recently torn through, has achieved a new apotheosis of chaos, crowned by his forgotten black felt hat on top of the bookcase. We're just like that, Matthew and I.

If *this* is love—and it is—then I can faintly glimpse what the love of God might be. So long as I understood it as a response to my pleasingness—*if* I was good, *then* God would love me (and contrariwise, if I was bad, then God would throw me into hell, the most hateful gesture imaginable)—I couldn't believe in it, since the chances of my ever being good enough to merit the love of God were slenderer than a strand of silk. But suppose God takes no particular delight in me at all. Suppose God finds me about as attractive as I found Matthew during the years when razorblades dangled from his ear and his room was littered with plates and glasses growing long green hairs and his favorite band was called Useless Pieces of Shit. Suppose God keeps me steadily in sight, agonizing over my drunken motorcycle rides and failed courses, laughing at my jokes, putting in earplugs and attending my gigs, signing for my release at the police station, weeping with me as we bury the dead dog…. Oh, I feel certain that she does.

Still, I'm not God, or anything like. I'm only a mother, and possibly a bad one at that. At least I was told so often enough. I never seemed to get anything right. When I returned to work a year after Matthew's birth, my mother accused me of deserting her grandchildren, and although she now acknowledges that it seems to have done them no harm, I was haunted throughout their childhood by the conviction that my professional life, which I believed I needed not just for the money but for my sanity, rendered me neglectful and selfish. By the time, fifteen years later, George's father condemned me for failing to make Matthew get a decent haircut and decent clothes and decent friends (clothes making the man and a man being known by the company he keeps), I was no longer willing to take the blame any more than I accepted praise for Anne's accomplishments. But I could have used a little praise for my own accomplishments. In the couple of decades that I had at least one child in the house, no one ever exclaimed, "Gee, Nancy, that was a nifty bit of mothering there!"

George least of all. He shared in the childcare from the outset, even changing "dirty" diapers (this always seemed to be held up as the mark of paternal devotion, that a man would muck about with his baby's shit), and his involvement excited admiration, at least from other women, especially me. No one would have said of me that I shared in the childcare, much less admired my generosity in sparing George some of the work. This was the sixties, and the lot fell to me. In fathering children, a man produced "mouths to feed," but the obligation was metaphorical: George had to make enough money to procure the strained peas, but no one expected him to pop the lid off the jar, spoon the glop into a rosebud mouth, and then block the spray before the kitchen took on the hue of the Owl and the Pussycat's boat. Nor was I admired for sharing in the task of pea-procurement. What was sauce for the gander was in those days definitely not sauce for the goose.

I am only pointing out the imbalance in gender expectations here, not denigrating George's participation in childrearing. He was an exceptional caregiver, attentive, companionable, humorous, at times unquestionably a better mother to the children than I, especially during the period when I really did abandon them, sinking into depression, moving out of the house, and attempting suicide. Ironically, however, this depression may have been triggered by his increasing remoteness, for as the children grew older he began to pull away from us all. Far from sharing in the childcare, now that the care entailed not bedtime baths and goofy games but sexual guidance, supervision of homework and chores, disciplinary action, he devoted all his energy to pea-procurement, not just for us but for the needy world beyond our door, and after a while, in secret, to Sandra, who sent her child away before he ever got there, providing him a tidy, tranquil refuge. Every family with adolescents must have a resident Big Meany, and he wasn't about to be It.

In his absence, I was forced into decisions only to have him stop by just long enough to undermine them. "Well, I wouldn't have done what you did," he'd say when I protested; it didn't occur to him to support my action, telling me that he disagreed with me, even asking me not to do it again, but seeing me through it once it was done. So certain did he appear of his essential rectitude on these occasions that I could never disagree with him without being made to feel—after a while a single stony glance would do the trick—foolish, guilty, difficult, mean, hysterical. Years later, when he finally began to open himself to me, he explained that his absences, silences, and contradictions had arisen not so much from self-righteousness as from uncertainty and confusion, which society did not permit him even to feel, much less to acknowledge. As an adult male, he was required to take command, do the right thing, or else lose face. Since he didn't know what to do with the children any more than I did but couldn't afford to betray his ignorance, he fled. Later, he could approve or disapprove my decisions; and since the disapprovals rankled, those are the ones I remember. But of course! Illuminated by this fresh knowledge, huge chunks of our past—baffling and bitter—fall into interpretable patterns.

Too late for the children, though, who have struck out into the world baring their birthright of bumbles and blunders. If only we could have them back as babies today, now that we have some idea what to do with them…. But no. They're so fine as they are that they don't need another go-round. Children must be designed to survive and transcend parental fault the way desert vegetation endures drought: Anne and Matthew aren't even spindly and scraggly. After two years in Zaïre teaching farmers how to raise fish for food, Anne returned to Tucson and married another Peace Corps Volunteer; she teaches composition while working toward a master's in teaching English as a second language, and Eric is earning a doctorate in biochemistry. Matthew and Poppy, who have been together since they were fifteen, were married last year; Poppy cares for a quadriplegic man, and Matthew, who plays rock and classical bass, has finished an associate's degree in music. Where there were once two children, now there are four, and I imagine that one day, there'll be even more, who will no doubt also endure and thrive while Anne and Eric and Matthew and Poppy dither through the fens and thickets, where George and I once lurched lost and footsore, emerging at last into this sunlit space, everyone—miraculously—accounted for and in one piece.

If parenthood taxed us so, you'd think George and I might have had the sense not to have any more children. And in truth we never intended to have more children. We were careful not to conceive again after Matthew's problematic birth and especially after my multiple sclerosis was diagnosed. Following a pregnancy scare, George volunteered to have a vasectomy. Although we weren't Catholics at the time, it wouldn't have mattered if we had been, since we believe that the Church's condemnation of birth control not only intrudes upon personal conscience but actually interferes with responsible behavior toward God's creation. Why would anyone want us to produce a damaged child or a child whose mother was too ill to care properly for her?

When young, I'd been told that Catholics under the direction of the pope conspired to take over the world through their continual breeding, but no one pointed out that the conspirators were rich white men in long dresses and beanies whereas the tools of conspiracy were women, most plentifully poor brown women staggering through their eighth, or twelfth, or twentieth pregnancies who prayed to the Blessed Mother of an only child (for so the Church insists) to send a little rice, a little beans, maybe a chicken for Sunday. The issue has never really been one of quantity but of control: not more Catholics but "good" Catholics, docile and too exhausted to resist the domination of those who claim (through the merits of a bit of flesh dangling between their legs that they're forbidden to touch) privileged access to God. A woman who controls something as essential as her own procreative processes might prove unbiddable in other matters as well. She might reach out to God directly; then what power would a mediator possess?

Through its prohibition on birth control, the Church has suggested that the only right way to have a family is through additional biological reproduction: a kind of forced labor culminating in the production of another soul for God. What kind of a God stands like Lee Iacocca at the end of an assembly line, driving his workers with a greedy "More! More!" while the automobiles pile up in showrooms and on freeways and in used-car lots and finally junkyards, his only satisfaction the gross production figures at the end of every quarter? The human race may once have needed conserving and augmenting through conception, pregnancy, and childbirth, but that project has succeeded rather too well. I've had a little experience in these matters (vastly more than the pope, the cardinals, the archbishops and the bishops, or your local parish priest, all of whom might benefit from a few good years of non-symbolic fatherhood), and I can tell you that there are all kinds of ways to have a family, no worse than the biological route and possibly better, since God requires not merely that we produce children but that we care properly for the ones already here. In a world of finite resources, this task may now necessitate voluntary limitations on reproduction.

I'm not proposing that we should call an abrupt halt to the birds and bees business. On the contrary, in spite of my bitching, I'm thrilled to have borne and raised Anne and Matthew. Personally, I've been forced into the kinds of growth I couldn't have experienced otherwise; and the world has gained two splendid presences. I wouldn't ask anyone to forgo such joy. But I do think that we should de-emphasize biology as the basis for forming authentic families. We should stop making those incapable of reproduction feel so guilty and deprived that they go to sometimes quite crazy lengths to get a baby in a socially acceptable form, a "real" baby. And we should encourage those who responsibly elect to produce only one or two offspring to ask themselves whether their family is quite big enough or whether it could benefit from just one more.

As for George and me, our habit has been to acquire new family members in their teens or early twenties, which saves on diapers and strained peas but offers its own sort of challenges. Childrearing may be demanding, difficult, even on occasion down right crazy-making, but at least if you've been in the company of this creature from the moment of conception (or, in the case of many adoptions, a few days after birth), you have had continual opportunity to adjust to its idiosyncrasies; in fact, you may be partly responsible for those idiosyncrasies. If the creature shows up on your doorstep at the age of twenty-one, some other mother may have adjusted beautifully to its idiosyncrasies but you most certainly have not. And all the good will in the world will not stop you from moments of wishing that that other mother had strangled it at birth. But in time you learn to accept these murderous fantasies as natural and let them drift through your conscious and on out into whatever ether safely holds all our murderous fantasies at a distance from our active lives.

Take our "youngest." When the little house in our backyard that I now use as a studio fell vacant in 1988, I wondered whether it might be useful to a shelter for battered women as a means of extending the stay of someone who needed more than the two or three weeks most shelters can offer before she struck out on her own. Liking the idea, George called the Tucson Shelter for Women and Children. The woman there was noncommittal, of course (who wouldn't be when some guy calls up looking for a woman to live in his little house?), but we've lived in the community long enough to be easy to check on, as she did, and shortly she suggested a young woman with a year-old baby. A baby? This is a little house, mind you. A little, little house. Just a room with a three-quarter bath and a closet. Of course, she'd have access to kitchen and laundry facilities in the "big" house, which is itself what many would call little, but her private space would be extremely cramped. But sure, she could come take a look. You can say this about acquiring children by this method: it doesn't take nine months, and it's painless. That very evening our family grew by two: Sylvia and Shane.

Not that we exactly knew what had happened right away. We'd offered shelter for a few weeks, which is time enough to begin a friendship but not to extend a family. When Sylvia said she needed a place until she finished business school in June, we suggested that she try it for a month; if she and Shane weren't totally squirrelly at the end of that time, she could stay on, paying us rent of a hundred dollars a month out of her welfare check. In this way, we hoped that she'd feel entitled to the space, not admitted to it at the sufferance of Lord and Lady Bountiful. Issues of dependence and self-sufficiency invariably arise with adult children, even children you don't yet recognize as yours, and we wanted Sylvia to understand that we believed her capable of providing for herself and Shane. She didn't always pay her rent on time, and sometimes she had to borrow some it of back, but on balance she met this responsibility fully.

Another thing about getting children this way: it's gradual. You can't be a little bit pregnant, and once you are pregnant, the condition doesn't generally escape your notice; but you may become a foster parent, at least in the informal way George and I have done it, in increments too small to distract you from whatever else you think you're doing at the time. The few weeks we'd offered in September stretched into nine months. Then the business school that had promised to train Sylvia and find her a terrific job by June persuaded her that she couldn't possibly find a *really* terrific job without more training, so she borrowed several thousand dollars more for tuition and signed on till March. This was a scam (as became clear when the school didn't even try to find her a job of any sort), but she was too insecure to resist, and suddenly nine months promised to be eighteen.

In the end, Sylvia was one of our family (but by no means the only one) who needed a nudge out of the nest. Well, more like a hearty heave. Although we gave her six months' notice, allowing her plenty of time to plan had she been so inclined, her circumstances had made her hesitant, timid. Because her divorced mother had never been well, their roles had often been reversed; Sylvia fled this burdensome relationship straight into the arms of a man even more childish; at the time she fled his beatings, she and Petey and five-month-old Shane were living in his car. Through a special program at the shelter, she'd stayed seven months instead of one, but seven months is not an adequate childhood. As part of our family, she could go on, for awhile, letting down her guard.

For me, Sylvia had come at a good time. Just a few months younger than Anne, who had gone off to Zaïre the year before, she was bright and affectionate. I was lonely for a daughter, someone to whom I could give pretty clothes and makeup and the quantities of gratuitous advice that had been building up like water on the brain. Although the little house was theirs, she and Shane spent most of their waking hours in the big one, and the presence of a toddler could be terrifically trying, but we were never burdened by his care. On the contrary, Sylvia relieved us of burdens, competently managing the household for us whenever we went away. And traveling is more fun when you've got children to take presents home to.

Sylvia finally graduated. After a couple of temporary and unsatisfactory living arrangements, she found an apartment for herself and Shane. Eventually she found a job, which she kept until the recession caused the firm to lay off two-thirds of its staff; then another, which she lost when she got pregnant again; now, she's back on public assistance, the father of this child no more inclined to provide for it than Petey was to support Shane. We feel as angry and disappointed as any parents would at her self-limiting behavior, but now seems the worst of times to reject her and Shane, and anyway, how could we get them out of our hearts? So we continue our intermittent phone calls and get-togethers. Each time Shane arrives, he seems another half head taller, too big really for the little chairs that were once Anne and Matthew's, but he drags one out and scrunches in it, chin on knees, as he brings us up to date on cultural developments we've missed, like Inspector Gadget and the Teenage Mutant Ninja Turtles, one of whom (I'm not sure which, but it can't have been Hieronymous Bosch or I'd remember) absolutely had to appear on the pair of shoes George took him to buy last week or else he would go barefoot from here to eternity.

"How many children do you have?" people ask, and I have to say, "Well, it depends on what you mean by children…." There are Ron and Angel and Alex and C.J. Anne and Eric. Matthew and Poppy. Sylvia and Shane and whoever the new baby will be. In time, these may produce even more, but George and I are in such fragile health now that I don't foresee our taking in any others from the outside. I'm not making any promises, though. Accidents happen.

Of late, a terrific hue and cry has been raised by political conservatives about "family values." Although the words are general to the point of inanity, few people ask for definitions specific enough to determine whether what a speaker means by "family" and "values" matches their own understanding. The followers of Charles Manson identified themselves as a family, after all; so strong is the religio-familial sense among the Mafia that they call their leaders "godfathers"; murder and mayhem may be just as highly prized as any other fun for the whole family. All the same, when some handsome blond politician of relatively few years and even fewer brains fulminates about the return to traditional "family values" in a sound bite on the nightly news, I know the family he has in mind: a daddy who works for wages outside the tidy white house with the two-car garage, a mummy who works for room and board inside it, two-point-something children, a fluffy cat and a spotted dog, and a cookie-baking grandma in a flowered apron who lives far enough away to render occasional visits a treat. Daddy hasn't lost his job in the copper mine, and Mummy has never attempted suicide. Dick hasn't just come out of the closet; Jane isn't scheduled to have an abortion in the morning; baby Sally wasn't born with cerebral palsy; the dog and cat have had their rabies shots; Grandma's intermittent lapses of memory don't signal the onset of Alzheimer's. And certainly a scrawny kid from a nearby detention center—no relation at all, not even a member of the same race—hasn't recently moved into the spare room and started classes at Dick and Jane's high school.

The millions of us who learned to read from the same primer all know the family, with its values of propriety and self-control, he envisions. But what can we make of his tone, so shrill and desperate that in a woman it might be called hysterical? What's he got at stake? "Expansive monarchs...valorized the patriarchal family," the historian Lois Banner writes," as representing in miniature the centralized state, thereby positioning the father in the family as akin to the male monarch heading the state." Once again, like Virginia Woolf in *Three Guineas* nearly sixty years ago, we uncover the complicity between the public and private spheres. In the absence of a throne, Handsome Young Politician may aspire to an expansive presidency: the United States dominating the family of man, just as our HYP heads the United States, just as each man in the United States carries out his rightful (even God-given) role as paterfamilias. Thus, he extols traditional family values not because these are inherently good (goodness being a culturally based attribute) but because they replicate the power relationships on which his status depends. What's at *stake?* Only the world as we know it!

Another man, dark-skinned, dark-eyed, even younger than our HYP and something of a political klutz, once suggested family might best not be based on blood ties at all. "My mother and my brothers," he said, "are those who hear the word of God and do it" (Luke 8:21): those who love God without restraint and their neighbors as themselves. The family, the microcosm into which we're born, inevitably serves as the model for our wider systems of relationships, and those of us who want a genuinely new world order—equitable, inclusive, tolerant, pacific, filled with jokes and festivals—must develop our ideas about family, and our families themselves, in the light of that correlation. There really is a human family (even in the genetic sense, our mitochondrial DNA having come to us through our mother all the way from some primordial Eve), for which we need a new family order. What's at stake here is not the-world-as-we-know-it, but the world. Period.

Toward this end, I must confess, the Mairs family, which is in most respects about as conventionally middle American as you can get, has taken only a couple of tottering steps, and for this reason, I sometimes hesitate to say much about us even as I long, through sharing our experiences, to encourage others to unfold and enrich their lives by opening their families as we have done. This is a tricky point, this matter of public disclosure, one on which Jesus isn't entirely helpful: "Beware of practicing your piety before men in order to be seen by them," he cautions, yet within the same sermon he says, "Let your light so shine before men, that they may see your good works and give glory to your Father who is in heaven" (Matt. 5–7). If I write about my hetero-dox motherhood, an act that I certainly intend to be "seen" by men, and women too, am I parading my piety, or am I providing them a chance to glorify the holy? Probably, my experience of Christian moral practice tells me, both. Just to be on the safe side, since I've always found self-righteousness at least as seductive as sex, I take Jesus literally: "No one is good but God alone" (Mark 10:18). Whatever you see in me, it's not piety.

I'm not being cute here, brushing aside my maternal life with a blush and a flick of the wrist: "Oh, pshaw, it's really nothing." Childcare is never *nothing*. I just don't see anything praiseworthy in doing no more than one believes one is required to do. On this point Jesus is perfectly explicit: "Whoever receives one such child in my name receives me"; and whoever "receives me, receives not me but him who sent me" (Matt 18:5, John 13:20). God has come here to me in the form of newborn infants and abandoned adolescents and unwed mothers, draped in chains and padlocks with a razor blade dangling from one ear, breaking my crockery, staining the floral chintz of my favorite couch, planting sticky kisses on my lips and eyeglasses, waving goodbye on the way to kindergarten, to boot camp, to Iceland or Africa. It is not a wonder that I have taken God in, but a scandal that I have received God so infrequently and grumpily. Nevertheless, God's house is commodious. Jesus has assured me, and when the time comes for her to return my dubious hospitality, I have every reason to believe that she, of all beings, can always find room for one more.

Embracing Life

"It was having the children," he told me.
"That's what broke your heart open."

— ROSEMARY BRAY McNATT

Jonathan Johnson

At Blackhorse Lake

The world is what it is. Right now, for example, the last day of October, not terribly cold wind is rustling the long dry grass and reeds along the shore of what's most accurately described as a small marsh under cumulous clouds on their way east through blue sky. The far horizon is pine in every direction and in the little bit of pond that's left at the center of a muddy margin there are six swans. They float a while, then stand, their bellies rising off the shallow, wind-rippled water, and flap their wings or arch their long necks over to work their beaks through their chest feathers. They settle back down and float. The clouds move over the sun, then the sun shows itself again, white on the spent duff of cattails along the tops of the reeds, even whiter on those swans.

It is almost too cold to sit outside writing. But the wind stills and a magpie passes, pulling its long tail through the air; and the sun gets half a chance to warm my scalp and the black fleece on my back and shoulders, and there's that solitary, broken-off pine trunk rising from the cattails and reeds, with bleached gray limbs. And amid all the pine and grass, there is one stand of aspen, yet another white—bone—and bare except for the faint shimmer of a very few brown leaves. In patches down close to the ground, with the dead pine needles and sticks, there is short grass that's not dry at all, but still green. It's been a warm autumn.

The world is what it is. Far beyond the curve of the earth, where evening is coming on by now, my mother died last winter. I couldn't tell you how many amputations she had, toes and then foot, shin and more shin bone, more toes and fingers knuckle to knuckle to nothing, the other foot, thumb. I've lost count. All of us love our private hyperboles. Here's mine: her surgeon, a friend, stood in my family's house two days after she'd died, drink in his hand and said he'd never seen a patient suffer so much.

Later, when the house was full, people on every chair and along the couch and standing and sitting on the floor, my wife spoke and told a story from two summers before. Our daughter, Anya, who was two years old at the time, sat in my mother's lap as my mother sat in her wheelchair at the bottom of the ramp that leads gently down from the deck to the backyard. (The mums there are long done by now, I suppose, the last of my mother's flowers to give up the year, and the birch, like these aspen, must be bare.) My mother still had one foot on the summer day my wife was describing—and she used it to push herself and my daughter backward up the ramp to the deck. Then she told Anya to hold on, lifted the foot and let the wheelchair roll down the ramp as they shouted with delight. They laughed at the bottom and Anya said, "Again Nana," and my mother obliged. My mother made my wife promise not to tell my father—the watcher and nurse of her open wounds, the one who knew what a fall could mean.

Of her cluster of diseases all that's worth saying is they were the kinds of things people get—diabetes combined with a not uncommon small-vessel and nerve condition called Raynaud's and a related thing called Crest scleroderma—nothing particularly exotic, no key words of dread. It was just that together they slowly took her extremities after years of allowing in occasional infections, the antibiotics from which finally destroyed her kidneys. When her palms and the few remaining nubs of her fingers turned purple and white and black, and our friend the surgeon said all that was left to do was take everything to just below both elbows, and he admitted there wasn't much chance she'd outlast the operation by long and the thrush in her mouth made it painful to talk, and the sores on her back and tailbone were raw to the flesh, and she was buried down under so many narcotics that it took great effort to climb to the surface and open her eyes and smile and say hello, she let go.

There was so much to let go. While her body was being carved away and more and more hours of her days were spent on the business of surviving, her life had kept growing. Movies, cappuccino with my father in the car parked overlooking the lake shore, her peonies and daylilies blooming (in the last few years when this or that finger was withered and bandaged and she could no longer dig in the dirt, I dug for her while she sat in her chair and supervised), and so much of Anya. Anya—"my little sprite" she called her—running naked out into the backyard. Anya in her lap in the wheelchair, Anya propped up in bed beside her in the morning, both of them drinking from cups with spill-proof lids and big handles. And during that week back in February, the week my mother's doctors said she'd have left when she stopped going to dialysis, Anya turning, arms stretched above her head, turning her dance from dance class for my mother, who had raised her head and lifted the unimaginable weight of her eyelids to see.

But the hardest thing for my mother about losing my daughter, I would guess, wasn't the reality of never seeing her again, impossibly hard as that must have been—that bright little face fading away with everything else. From what I know of my mother, what was hardest about losing Anya was that there would be no more days to teach her. Anya is four now (or, as she'd correct me, "four and a *half*, Daddy"), and though some of how she'll feel about her life has, I suppose, been settled by now, much of the quality of her relationship to her life still remains an open question, I know.

As her father I also know there's only so much I can do to effect what comes her way in that life. I'll work to preserve places like this little marsh of a lake for her, I'll teach her to be good to her body and spirit, to tend herself and surroundings with attentiveness. But precious little of what will be the tangible world for Anya is up to me. Or her. The lesson my mother taught my daughter in the days they had together was not how to change the world. The lesson she taught and the lesson I must now keep teaching for her—the lesson I'm determined she'll keep teaching through me—is how to be at home in the world.

The world is what the world is, and my mother loved it. Orphaned at sixteen, growing up to live what now seem so few healthy years, then for years enduring a body that slowly died from without, she loved to hold leaves in her hand, loved the way the seagulls walked, the voices of the geese passing low, the opportunity to speak kind words to someone for whom kind words may have been rare. What I get from being Anya's father and my mother's son, the specific purpose the two of them together give my life, is this: a duty to look on every day of this life as an opportunity for love. You can only teach what you know. And it is perhaps through teaching that you come to know something deepest in your soul.

The wind picks up and I can feel it pushing on the car where I've taken refuge. It subsides and I roll down the window and can hear it like steady breath through thousands of pine needles. It picks up again, and the tall grass shuffles and tilts and crowds.

She knew how it could hurt, but my mother loved this world more purely and unconditionally than anyone I've known. "I have a good life," she said many times over the years, planting her emphasis on "good" so deep in my memory I hear her clearly now. That and, "You don't get the days back." When she answered the phone nearly every night for the last six years and it was my sister calling from one or another far-off city to tell about her latest struggle or latest joy and talk about her next trip home, my mother loved the world. When I held a rose blossom in my cupped hands to her nose during that last week and she could only smile and not open her eyes she loved the world. And when she still couldn't open her eyes, as my sister and father and I swabbed her sores clean as gently as we could and sang "Under the Boardwalk" and she whispered, "Sounds good," she loved the world. And on that last day, propped up with pillows and every breath a fight through clenched teeth, when she opened her eyes and managed to say, "Help me," she loved the world. I know, because then, her eyes still looking into my eyes, she said, "I love you." Her last words.

The pine trees' shadows are getting long across the grass and their needles quiver gold in the sunlight. I have work to do. This world is what it is, and I must love it. I must love it, and I must teach Anya to love it—a responsibility that is not just a reason to go on, but the greatest good fortune of my life.

We drive out to this place together sometimes—lately to find and identify scat. We lean over some coyote or elk or goose's poop and poke it with our sticks and look for tiny bones and fur or the empty skins of berries. Lately, we've seen the animals themselves, these swans, an eagle, a coyote, elk, a porcupine shuffling along. Anya picks up pieces of moss and bark and little stones (but thus far no scat) to take home for her collection. We have guide books to tell us the names of things, and we look them up. But mostly we just hold and look at them as one would with gifts from a beloved. As I expect she will this wonderfully long, hollow shaft of some kind of grass I've broken off and will bring home to her now, token of this world as it is. What my mother gave us.

Cora Schenberg

A Theory of Falling Bodies

How's this for an introduction to a class on Genesis: the professor hands each student an apple.

"Close your eyes," she says, "and remember the happiest moment of your life. Now imagine yourself back in that moment. Now, imagine you have a choice. You may opt to stay in your moment forever. Should you do so, time will stand still. You will not age; anyone alive now will not die. If you are pregnant, you will stay pregnant forever. The weather will never change.

"Your other choice is, you may eat your apple. In which case, you will move on from your moment, leave paradise. You and others will age and die, experience all varieties of weather, all aspects of life."

If given the choice, I'd forgo my apple. I'd let time freeze on October 30, 1999. My friend Elaine got married on that day. Here is a picture of the whole party: bride and groom in the center, surrounded by bridesmaids, groomsmen, and the obligatory kids, flower girl and ring bearer.

In our snapshot, Mary, the maid of honor, stands to the left of the bride. She is all smiles. She has all her hair. Five months after the wedding, Mary will be dead, her hair lost to chemotherapy treatments. On that October day, she does not know she has cancer. If I could stop time, Mary would still be here. If I could stop time, Dan, the bridegroom, would not have lost his job and fallen into a severe depression three months after the wedding. He would be as he is in the photograph: grinning as he towers over his bride. The bridesmaid to the bride's right is pregnant with her second child, just beginning to show. I am that bridesmaid, and if I could stop time, I would not miscarry two weeks from the day of this wedding.

This is the story of that child who was not to be.

It is late on a Friday afternoon in September. I am at home, preparing for our family's Sabbath, or Shabbat. Although we are not Orthodox, my family and I keep Shabbat regularly. Every Friday afternoon I buy my challah on standing order from a local bakery. Sometime before evening falls, I turn off my computer and do no writing until Saturday evening. My family and I say blessings over candles, wine, and bread. As often as possible we have guests. We do this not only because it is fun, but also because in doing so we keep two commandments: making Shabbat and welcoming people into our home.

Tonight is Erev Rosh ha-Shana, the eve of the Jewish New Year, as well as Shabbat. Our guests are my friend Shira and her three children, who are friends of our four-year-old son, Gabriel. After dinner, my husband, Wade, and I serve challah and apples dipped in honey, a wish for a sweet New Year. Then we all go to temple to pray with the community; afterward, we hug our friends and wish them "Shana tova," a good year. We linger outside the temple. Although it is September, it feels like late May. The perfect night to conceive a second child.

I should explain, because I am proud of this. We Jews are not an ascetic people. It is actually a mitzvah, a commandment, to make love with your spouse and a double mitzvah to do so on Shabbat. If a child is conceived in the process, what could be better? So after we put Gabriel to bed, I pray that God will bless us.

Two weeks later, it has happened: a positive pregnancy test. To say I am ecstatic would be a gross understatement. The next day Wade and I take Gabriel out to lunch.

"Mommy is going to have a baby," Wade tells him.

"Good!" says Gabriel.

It is a hard pregnancy, harder than with Gabriel, but that's okay. Everyone says there is a much lower incidence of miscarriage among women who have morning sickness than among those who don't. I repeat this as a mantra since I feel pretty green most of the time.

It is a strangely warm fall, eighty-five degrees during the days. Gabriel runs around the yard in his shorts and sandals while I work in the garden. Gardening takes my mind off morning sickness like nothing else.

Then there is Elaine's wedding to plan for. Mary and I organize the shower, get our dresses—which we both hate but agree to wear anyway because we love the bride. Mary drives Gabriel and me to the wedding, talking cheerfully on the way about her upcoming nurse practitioner boards, her sister-in-law's pregnancy. It's a perfect wedding, a warm, sunny day. Perfect pictures: bride and groom kiss; bride embraces maid of honor; ringbearer (Gabriel) walks down the aisle. I *do*. Click. Freeze!

Freeze, goddamn it!

Two weeks later, I am storming through the house, kicking Legos and toy trains out of my path. "This house is a mess," I yell. "Gabriel, when will you stop leaving your toys where people can trip on them? And great. You've pooped your pants again. Wade, can you take over? Please? I'm going to services."

That's right, going to pray. Set my mind right, get back to God. It's Shabbat. What's wrong with me, anyway?

At Hillel House, my friend Sonia greets me. She offers a warm hug, asks how I'm feeling, compliments my new shape.

I love Sonia. I love many of the others at Hillel House, but everything is wrong. Goddamn new-age services. Why are these people smiling? I should have gone to the temple instead. An *om* in Jewish Saturday morning worship? That does it; I'm out of here.

Out, but go where? The flea market? Nothing there I want. Latte? No, everything tastes terrible. What the hell is wrong with me?

The fact is, I hate everything but my husband.

"I'm at the end of my rope," I tell him that evening. "I'm happy to be pregnant, but damned tired of feeling sick all the time, and I hate my food tasting like poison. And I can't stand having this damn thing around my neck!"

I practically rip off the beautiful pendant Wade gave me for our fifteenth anniversary last year. It's in the shape of a mezuzah, a Jewish ornamental prayer scroll used to remind us of the presence of God.

Twenty-four hours later, I need no reminder.

What I need is a new law of physics. When I was little, I learned the Law of Falling Bodies from a story about Galileo. In the story, Galileo climbs to the top of the Tower of Pisa, drops a ten-pound sphere and a one-pound sphere, and watches as the two land at the same time. Well, it's just that: a story, both apocryphal and scientifically inaccurate. The only way the two objects would have landed simultaneously would have been if they had fallen in a vacuum.

But now I need to account for falling bodies. I see blood, just a few drops. As a mother-to-be, I've never asked what holds the seed of new life in place in my womb, never feared the hold might be precarious.

Is my baby falling? I am hurtled into space; I keep gulping, can't get air.

"Light bleeding, Cora?" My midwife, Kelly, asks over the phone. Her voice is an oasis of calm. "You're probably okay, but for peace of mind, why don't you come in tomorrow morning, and we'll listen for the heartbeat. All right?"

Sure, but should I lie down now? Put my feet up? According to Newton's Law, gravity pulls objects toward the earth, but can't a mother prevent that by putting her feet up? That's where my science turns out to be apocrypha; Kelly says if the baby has started to abort, it's already dead. "But you're probably okay," she reminds me. "I'll see you tomorrow, first thing."

We're probably okay. And now the bleeding has stopped. Reassured, I get a good night's sleep.

But in the morning it's back. Red flag. Hard to breathe. Wade holds me, helps me ready Gabriel for school. Breakfast, brush teeth, prayers. I try to thank God for life in my belly, but the words stick in my throat.

"Sometimes in this early phase it's hard to pick up the heartbeat," says Kelly, removing the Doppler from my stomach. "Let's go see what the ultrasound can tell us."

A few minutes later, Kelly says, "Cora, I see your little baby, and I'm afraid it's not moving."

Dr. Newman comes in, looks at the screen carefully, takes in the baby from different angles; says, simply, "No."

Jews have a blessing for every occasion. You heard good news? Say, "Praised are You, God, who is good and beneficent." Someone has died? You say, *"El dayyan emet,"* God is a true judge, acknowledging the rightness of all God does, even that which feels horribly wrong. Jewish law also mandates that a mourner tear the garment she's wearing closest to her heart, to reflect the sundering caused by death.

I rip at my shirt and cry, *"El dayyan emet!"*

"You have options," Kelly tells me gently.

My baby is dead, and I have options. I can wait for the fetus to abort itself, or I can have surgery.

"No," says Dr. Newman for the second time. "I wouldn't wait in your case. This baby is too big; you could hemorrhage."

I ask for immediate surgery, but the doctor's schedule is packed. I'll have to wait until Wednesday. This is Monday.

I now have to tell a story about blood. It's woman's blood. In commercials, they talk about feminine hygiene, pour clear or blue liquid on sanitary napkins to show their absorbency. Anything but red.

Much of the time, a woman's blood heralds life. The menstrual flow prepares her body for conception. At birth, the child announces its arrival with a splash of red.

We don't talk about this. So how to talk about my blood? It is Monday afternoon. My friend Debbie and I are drinking tea on the couch when I feel the spurt between my legs. This blood announces the coming of the child, but not joyful childbirth: my body is a graveyard. This blood laughs in the face of a doctor who said wait till Wednesday, his schedule is packed. This blood carries away my baby's soul; I feel my baby's soul leave me, and I tell my baby, it's okay, you go home to God. I love you. But it's not okay; I only want you with me, my soul. *El dayyan emet.*

Then Wade is home, Gabriel is packed off in the car with Debbie and her children, and Wade and I go to the emergency room. Martha Jefferson Hospital, where Gabriel was born. We have to wait, and wait more. The lights are too bright, room too sterile, and I'm scared. I read psalms for a house of mourning, daven evening prayers. Someone takes blood, someone else puts in an IV. This is where I have to say good-bye.

"Can't I bury the baby myself?" I ask the doctor.

"No," he says. After he's used his vacuum extractor, well, there won't be much left to bury.

Like Galileo's mythic spheres, we do not fall in a vacuum. Once home from the hospital we call Wade's parents. They are with us by the next day; when they leave, my mother arrives and takes over. Friends from temple make us a beautiful memorial service. Just when I decide I need a book of psalms in Hebrew and English, a friend brings one.

My friend Jean, a poet, suffered two miscarriages and never had a child. She knows grieving. "It's a very orderly process," she tells me. "You don't have to do anything, just let it carry you."

I do, and it is. There are times designated—not by me—to cry, eat, sleep, pray, write, wake up, and cry more. Toward the end of that first week, I know the baby's name: Ori, Hebrew for "my light." I do not name the baby but inexplicably learn the name, and then cry again, realizing whom I've lost. I go through the process, discover the truth about falling bodies: they need only surrender to the fall.

Two weeks pass, and I find myself back in the world, where almost no one knows the truth about falling bodies. Instead, people spout absurdities:

"Next time, have your husband help you garden when you're pregnant."

"There must've been something wrong with that baby. It was probably retarded."

"It wasn't meant to be." (This said in a maddening, sing-song voice.)

"You can try again."

"Next time, don't get so attached to it."

And here it is Friday afternoon. Normally, dinner would be coming along in preparation for Shabbat. But tonight I have no idea what we will eat; we have invited no guests. Instead of being home, cooking, I am at a playground with Gabriel. But am I really with him? He is full of imaginative games. We found Tarzan behind a tree; the play structure turned into a space ship. I pretended to get the moon for Gabriel, who is now floating in outer space.

As am I. Much as I know I am tethered to the world, as the astronaut is to his ship, I don't feel part of the world now.

"We landed at Jupiter!" Gabriel tells me. Yes. He's now gathering rocks for a moon festival. He piles some in front of my park bench.

I believe in God, and in the connection between all forms of life, tenuous as it may seem at times. It is a delightful challenge, at this moment, to imagine this connection. A fence separates our playground from a major highway; as I sit, cars race past, each carrying stories that could fill 10,000 pages. Shadows are falling. It will soon be Sabbath for my family. Time to park the car, stop racing around.

After dinner at a pizzeria, we go home and set up the Shabbat candles, cover the challah, say the blessings. I read Gabriel his bedtime stories, tuck him in. Then I change clothes for temple. I need time with God. My faith is still intact but is tarnished by anger, obscured by fear of what God can do. In a neighboring pew sits Linda, a smart, compassionate woman in her sixties. Her daughter has had four miscarriages and a stillbirth. "When will it stop?" I ask God.

And while I've got God's attention, what about my resentment of pregnant women, particularly those due in early June as Ori was? Here is Emily in the pew behind me, her belly blossoming. I challenge God to teach me to embrace my lot, and let others have theirs, without rancor. *Hineni*, here I am. I am falling. Show me You are there.

I arrive home to find Wade and Gabriel asleep, the Sabbath candle almost completely burned. I put away the challah and its cover and plate.

So, *Adonai*, my God, who gives and takes away life: my family has made you a Sabbath, of sorts. A strange Sabbath, but I guess You're used to that, what with people plagued by war, disease, and death, people who weep tears into their challah. I thank You for all the Shabbat evenings where I have been able to speak of You, as the psalmist says, not just with awe, but "with vast joy." Tonight's is not much of a Sabbath, but it is what we have to give You.

About that apple, I'm relieved no one has offered it. What if someone gave me that choice years ago? Perhaps I'd have frozen time before my father's death, and would not have lost him. But neither would my son have come into the world. And as for freezing time before my miscarriage, pregnancy is not meant to be permanent. Mary's death is a harder one; she was a vital young woman, a wonderful friend. If I could keep her around by not eating an apple, I would.

How must Adam and Eve have felt, leaving the Garden after eating their apple? Cast out, naked, they did not know where to turn, or what would become of them. But then perhaps they

tasted more apples and realized how delicious they were.
    I step outside Elaine's wedding photo, into what comes next.

D.S. Butterworth

Ordinary Time

Moments of inspiration and vision, when the tree becomes a blaze of light or the rook shines incandescently, are rare and to be prized, but most of the time glimmers of the numinous arrive through the more mundane circumstances of the unexceptional. While the conventional search for the transcendent might lead into the mountains, through the woods, across rivers and the oceans they drain into, the ordinary just happens, down here where most of us live in the everyday, the truly secret place the poets teach us to stop taking for granted. And it is this ordinary that lifts its dust on occasion to point us toward what we can scarcely talk about without pushing further from us, without damaging—the ultimate things.

Our ordinary is a dark mahogany table we bought in the Appalachian foothills of Kentucky. The wood has a luster that's broken by its grain like the crazing of an old oil painting. Reflecting off its deep burnt-honeyed surface could be winter light's chromatics of snow and shadow lifted by a sky of cerulean blue, or summer's dappled hues of sycamore. This is a place where the music of family life is conducted by plate and spoon two or three times a day: a sundial, the seasons rotating around the meals so fast we sometimes feel ourselves disintegrating into spun sand and ash, so fast we must hold onto our chairs to prevent time from sweeping us away entirely. But the times spent here, the meals

that comprise our domestic offices, provide us with our understanding of who we are and form the ground of our being. And
they do this with none of the sweep of a grand journey over the
mountains or oceans, with little of the lyricism of poetry, or the
maxims of philosophy.

Rather, they are full of the actual in which a little girl admon-
ished for picking her nose and putting her finger in her mouth
replies, *Dad, I'm only recycling,* in which we field questions about
whether or not trees eat bushes, and where the question, *What do
you want to be when you grow up?* is answered in all seriousness:
A truck! Lately what occurs here begins with a bored litany about
what did or didn't happen at school, with automatic answers to
questions about whether or not homework was turned in or tests
were given back or who they ate lunch with.

At times we move into deeper waters during the meal—one
daughter teaches us that lettuce has a fine skin, a transparent
meniscus she peels meticulously and lays on her lips to give them
a frosty sheen. She surprises us with what she calls teeter-totter
eyes, as she blinks at us in rapid fire alternation that resembles
nothing so much as a seizure. At times odd trivia from the newspapers and from school points to a world beyond, that we eat three
spiders a year in our sleep, that scientists have found an object in
space that appears to contain more energy than all other sources
of light combined, that two-headed salamanders have been discovered in a swamp in Louisiana. But this is to be expected at a table
where, when they were much younger, I would point to the chan-
delier and suggest that it was a Christmas tree, a mountain, a bird,
inviting their shrieks of protest, and encouraging, without knowing it, the after dinner parade in which the two of them stomped
and raised their arms like greedy trolls as they chanted *D Dessert,
D Dessert, D Dessert,* Sesame Street Muppets gone haywire.

That the table in our culture is the center of religious sacrament and ministry is clear, but that this persists in *our* house, even
though we don't go to church, or even as a habit say grace, is less
so, because we don't draw attention to it, sensing that to name the

ineffable risks diminishing it. This just seems to be the way our family works, by spiritual intuition rather than religious practice. Still, the table is a daily reminder of what the stakes are in the game of life, what could be lost through a split-second miscalculation of one or another driver on the freeway, for example. And so it becomes the yardstick of the degree to which I have let go and let my daughters fend for themselves in the world. While this seems necessary for the family to function, it also describes the natural growth from distrust to trust, from denying life to affirming it.

Popular images of spirituality, what people often seem to mean when they refer to the practices of particular faiths—nuns in pious prayer, Muslims bowing down toward Mecca, or televangelists holding their hands up in front of swaying congregants— suggest to me that spiritual life is conventional, mechanical, and constrained. But they also suggest what we mean when we talk about the spiritual—that there is a transcendent other, that we do or should want to know it, and that we must figure out how to approach it. Do we wait, watch, ask, or implore?

In the medieval poem *Gawain and the Green Knight*, King Arthur must hear, see, or partake of an adventure before he will sit down to eat, and so serves as the institutional memory of what it takes to be a knight. He's the one who understands that unless someone remembers what it means to be a hero, the society founded upon it will dissolve. I often think of that as I sit down to dinner, knowing that if I put it so bluntly eyes will roll and the teenagers' psychic doors will shut. But with our little foursome we don't have to remember, we have to anticipate. Arthur's ritual remembrance is met with the Green Knight who offers an axe blow for an axe blow, and everyone in the court senses there will be hell to pay for agreeing to his challenge, especially when the Green Knight picks up his head after he's lost it, and walks away. Gawain's journey of rediscovery takes him away from home and into the wilds. Our adventures take place between reaching for the salt and the passing of the bread.

"She has a pretty name," the older daughter said, of the name *Ellen.*

"Sure." Pretty enough, I thought, and eyed the salad.

It had been a long day. Getting college students excited about Gawain was itself a trial, far harder than it should have been. Midterm grades were due and my wife and I, both swamped with papers to grade, were in the daze induced by reading many thousands of words in those papers striving to be understood. I mentioned an article I had read in the waiting room at the dentist's about a phenomenon of sensory overlap, where one sensory experience conjures up another one. We knew the term *synaesthesia* as a poetic device, famously used in Stephen Crane's *Red Badge of Courage*, where he refers to the trumpet's "red blare," so the idea was not new to us. But we couldn't get over the fact that people actually had synaesthesia, like a condition, or a capacity, whereby they saw different geometrical shapes when they heard certain sounds, or saw different colors for different musical notes, or saw a particular color for each different letter of the alphabet.

"That's the one I have," she said. "Numbers too."

My wife and I looked at each other and then looked at her. She'd always been "artistic," her walls plastered with drawings and paintings that fought for space with posters of Jimi Hendrix, John Lennon, Billie Holiday, and Incubus. Her room was littered with the evidence: the easel, the paints, the ersatz palettes made out of paper plates, the sketchbooks strewn over the floor making it look like a crime scene demanding investigation.

"What do you mean?"

"You know, how *a* is red, and *b* is turquoise-ish green, and *c* is orange, and *d* is lime-green—"

"Hold on!" I said and got pen and paper. "Okay."

"*E* is lemony-yellow, *f* chocolate brown, *g* gingery brown, *h* forest green, *i*, either silver or light, cloudy sky gray, *j* medium brown, *k* yellow or cantaloupe…"

She continued to the alphabet's end and then began to list numbers. "Sometimes the colors blend and become a mix of the two, like paints, and together within words different colors take over and change other ones, so that gray can be silver in certain words, and like that."

"And how long has this been going on?"

"Always. *Ellen*," she explained, "the colors are autumn leaves."

We let this sink in.

"What is the prettiest word?"

"Violet."

She pointed out that her alphabet had no blue in it, though the number 2 was blue. The name *Annie* was rather bright, and *Elvis* was just like the person: silver, gold, and bronze.

It may not seem to follow that this would make it easier in the next couple of years to do a series of things I considered unimaginable just months before, but it did—letting her, my teenaged synaesthete, get into a car driven by a sixteen-year-old boy, or watching her drive down the street alone her first time, going on with my work as she heads off into the dark of the freeway to dance lessons, or buying a plane ticket for her to visit her friend in Portland. These routine rites of passage for a father are all predicated on the hope that the child's resourcefulness will surpass his fears, which shifts the dynamic by which we approach the spiritual from one of imagination to one of faith. Parents have been learning to let go for ages; it has rarely been easy, but the successes are the rule rather than the exception, however difficult, however intensely felt. But does this letting go amount to a spirituality?

If spirituality means the acknowledgment of a higher power and the desire to figure out how to approach it, then this letting go, for someone like me, amounts to a hope that slowly becomes trust, and then faith, proceeding subtly, like intuition. This is my synaesthesia: just as violet is conjured by a letter, so too the transcendent is conjured by my daughter moving beyond my sphere. This may be a spirituality of approximation and association, but it feels more real to me than the codified doctrines of religious faith. When I see that my daughter has an experience richer than

I could have imagined, I affirm that she is in good hands, better hands than mine. While we can debate over how to conceive of and what to call the force behind the personification, I am content to think of it as life, as the real, as God. It is easy for me to let go if that means accepting that my daughter enters into something extending far beyond my ability to imagine in complexity, variety, and beauty.

There's another term for this "letting go" that I've recently learned from a Catholic priest, a term that describes the basis of my religious life, which I prefer not to think of as religious at all, the term *surrender*. The images I see of religious effort arc images of discipline, effort, and piety, as if we can *make* the spiritual happen, through good works or good behavior, what at Assumption Catholic Grade School was called Deportment on the report cards I received for eight years. To truly surrender, my friend the priest says, is to give up control, and by so doing, to live in cooperation with the current of life. Because the adherence to the monolithic doctrines of Catholicism always seemed to me to run counter to a devotion to God, amounting to a sort of false idolatry, I am all the more moved by something as simple and extraordinary as my daughter's synaesthesia, which tells me that the world is marvelously diverse beyond my imagining, and it's in this mercurial wonder that spirituality is sometimes born.

But if the world can surpass our imaginings in this way, it can do so in others. There's a story we sometimes tell at the table about our younger daughter on the waters of Mutiny Bay in Puget Sound, about how she and a neighbor boy pushed a rubber dinghy from shore without oars. With the logic of second graders eager to get to the float a few dozen yards out in the bay, they assumed they could paddle with their hands. But the current was fast, the water deep, and they soon drifted past the float and down the bay, the familiar houses receding behind them at an alarming pace. We had come to make light of her chagrin and regret, of her rescue by a woman down the beach who rowed out to retrieve the wayward dinghy. And in the same way as our daughter mentioned her synaesthesia, the younger daughter mentioned how surprised she'd been that the water was so cold. I have been overly fond of pointing out that the water in the bay is so cold that it is virtually unswimmable, rarely rising above 50 degrees even in summer. That things turned out well makes it something we return to. It's a happy story, frightening only because we know enough to realize that sometimes the children on such waters don't come back.

But the last time we revisited it, when my daughter said that about the water being so cold, I thought to ask, "What do you mean, the water was so cold?"

"Well, I got in it."

"You got in the water?"

"Yeah. To try to push the boat to shore. We didn't have any oars. How else were we going to get to shore?"

Suddenly, we could feel her struggle to hold on to the side of that inflatable dinghy, chastened to know that the ordinary breaks open to reveal what it will, testing our faith that life has meaning in the fullness of its shape, including in its end. In the boat she'd been safe, but that she'd gotten into the water sent a shiver through us all, and the table grew quiet.

Having kids is not the most original thing to do in the world, a friend of mine used to say. And it's not that this is a simple corrective to solipsism. The poet William Blake wrote that *eternity is in love with the productions of time,* an idea which for me captures the point. Just as eternity blooms through the details of the moment's flowering, so too the ultimate is expressed through the here and now. It can't really be any other way. While we can never simply abandon our children to whatever comes their way, we have to learn to accept that their survival and thriving, however much they seem to remain within the sphere of our influence, extend beyond the parent's designs. If one of the attributes of God is true omnipresence, then spirit may be at work through it all, through the elements, the inspiration in a child's mind, the temperature of the water, the woman down the beach.

Of course, there are thousands of such moments each week, so many that I can only have faith that life goes on without me, and that is what my daughters have brought me to affirm. I have to believe that while there is a place for piety, real devotion can just as readily arise out of attentiveness to the particular commonplaces of our lives, and surely God must be deeply excited by quantum physics, a flourish in a Beethoven symphony, a guitar lead by Jimi Hendrix, pasta with wild mushroom sauce, the smell of urban alleys on hot days, a splash of color across a dull page, the migrations of cedar waxwings. This attention to the world may be the only reasonable purpose for being here, even granting the extravagant irrationality creation seems to suggest about the creator.

In the church that I have left there is a tradition of feast days that provides an alternative to the usual days, called the ordinary times, the times when nothing special happens except for all the living that gets done between the days remembered because somebody died on them. That's where we dwell and find the movements of spirit, in the little hours, the sound of dishes and glasses, where milk spills and tests get parents' signatures, where we ask what the plans are for the weekend, where the music of the now drifts from their rooms.

We eat and talk with a mindfulness, watching for the days when we will be apart, following the shadows as they glide across the table. When I was the age my elder daughter is now I concluded that my being here was inscrutable, that concentrating on the hereafter to discern the shape of our destination was somehow to miss the point. Forming my own ideas or conforming to others' notions about those ends substitutes a human design for what might be, or perhaps must be, beyond human construction. And so the only sure thing is to attend to the now. A friend likes to say that when it comes to faith, just as important as belief is the desire to believe. Faith then, too, may operate like synaesthesia, whereby the words that describe the incidents of our lives mean what they mean but also excite a splash of color that signals something that lies beyond.

Without trying we fall into the ordinary, where I trust that, even though there will come a time when my own children won't come back, it will be all right, because through our letting go they will have learned to hold on tight. We meet again at another meal where, situated against the grain of today, the objects on the table open up the secret heights of the mountainside, the seasons spinning around us, my daughters carrying on despite me, a name being pretty in more than sound, waters running deep and cold through the world.

Jess Walter

Saved

I went to church for the free cookies.

Every Sunday, I watched the neighbor kids, the seven scruffy Fredricksons—Sherman, Sis, Billy, Porky, Betty Jean, Val, and Jobe—climb aboard a blue school bus that took them to a mysterious church where they got to eat as many cookies as they could fit into their mouths. We'd just moved to the neighborhood and Sherman was my only friend: wiser about boobs, BB guns, and everything else of value to a ten-year-old boy. One day while we scavenged for cigarette butts in the field behind my house, Sherman looked up suddenly and asked if I was "saved."

Saved? Saved from what?

Sherman explained that Jesus saved people, and that the church with free cookies was where He did it. Sherman had seen this happen. In fact, a few months earlier, he had been saved. He lit up an unfiltered butt and blew a perfect smoke ring. So did I want to go to his church? I probably would've said yes without the cookies. I was ten, at my third new school in three years. I wore black-rimmed glasses and was the smallest boy in my class. No one needed saving more than me.

We weren't churchgoers, but that Sunday my parents let me follow Sherman onto the blue school bus ("Praise Jesus!" stenciled on the side), and we sang, "Michael Row the Boat Ashore" as we rumbled and bounced to a vacant grocery store in a strip mall a few miles away. The church was only for kids, like a Sunday day care for poor families. Blue school buses arrived from bad neighborhoods all over town, bearing rowdy, dirty kids like the truant roundup from *Pinocchio*.

They sat us on the carpeted floor of the empty store—dozens of us, writhing like snakes in a basket. The kids who brought recruits got to stand and introduce their guests. "This is my friend Jess," Sherman said. "He's here to get saved." There was a loud cheer. Then the pastor stood. He had slick black hair and teeth as big and white as piano keys. He talked about "knowing Jesus" and "accepting Jesus" and "inviting Jesus" into our hearts. He led us in prayer.

Then he handed out a comic book that colorfully depicted a red goat dancing on its hind legs in front of a lake of fire filled with children writhing in excruciating pain as their burning skin fell away from their bones.

"If you have not been baptized," the pastor said, "you will burn in hell. And if your family has not been saved, they will burn alongside you in hell for all of eternity."

Finally, he passed around a tub of cookies.

That night, when I closed my eyes, all I could see was my brother and sister and I boiling in that fiery pool. Hell smelled like Yellowstone Park. My parents were there too, shrinking beneath the beady red eyes of that goat. I cried until my mom came to the side of my bed.

I told her all about the Cookie Church, about the pastor and the comic book, about how my family was going to burn in hell because we weren't saved. Her big watery eyes took in my face. She covered her mouth with those long, thin fingers—my fingers now. "Oh, honey," she said finally. "Don't worry. We've all been baptized."

"We have? Even me?"

"Of course," she said. "When you were a baby."

"So I'm saved."

"Of course you are."

She said I couldn't go to that church anymore.
"The cookies weren't even very good," I whispered.
She sat by my bed until I fell asleep.

I grew up a chronic seeker. I read the Bible, studied the Upanishads and gleaned bits from the Tao te Ching. I pondered the Three Marks of Existence, the Four Noble Truths, the Five Constants, and the Eightfold Path to Nirvana. I have been a refrigerator Buddhist (koans magneted next to lunch menus and kids' pictures), a conversational Hindu, and an attendant of at least six different denominations of Christian church.

Yet I believe in nothing.

At least, I believe in nothing that can't be proven. I am hopelessly skeptical, heartlessly empirical. Even when I was sampling sacred texts, my response to them was as a critic, not a believer. I reveled in the poetry and paradox of the Old Testament and in the sublime simplicity of the Katha Upanishads, but in the end, these were just stories, no more infallible to me than *Great Expectations*, no wiser than *The Brothers Karamazov*. When I close the book, the characters tend to go away. Even God.

If I believe in anything, it is our primordial compulsion to tell such stories. Joan Didion fairly described the structure of this belief system in *The White Album*: "We tell ourselves stories in order to live.… We look for the sermon in the suicide, for the social or moral lesson in the murder of five.… We live entirely, especially if we are writers, by the imposition of a narrative line upon disparate images."

This is my religion then, the belief in our deep need to impose "a narrative line upon disparate images." In my novel *Land of the Blind* I created an atheist sinner who is compelled to confess. So he goes to the police. When the cop begins to realize there might not be a crime at the end of this confession, she suggests that the sinner might want to talk to a priest, that he might want to confess his sins to God. The sinner responds: "I don't believe in God… I believe in the police."

I love stories that ponder questions of spirituality but I think the answers are basically unknowable. I guess this makes me an agnostic, or maybe just an atheist who lacks confidence in his own skepticism. For a while I considered myself a Jainist, the ancient East Indian agnostic followers of "the Doctrine of Maybe," just so I could say that *I was something*. But a true Jainist practices vegetarianism and vows to do no harm to any being or object, respects not only plants and animals but also rocks and sticks.

Turns out I love bacon too much and sticks too little to be a true Jainist.

So I trudge along, blissfully unaffiliated—free agent, hapless explorer, jolly skeptic, profligate bet-hedger, cosmic shrugger. And when some well-meaning evangelical asks if I am a Christian, one day I hope to have the courage to say: Nope. I'm a novelist.

Later this year, just before my fortieth birthday, my oldest daughter, Brooklyn, will turn twenty, and I will wake up having been a father longer than I was not one. Brooklyn is a sophomore in college now, the same age her mother and I were when we retroactively failed our sex-ed classes and got pregnant. For some people, I think, young parenthood is a fairly natural state. I, however, was a moron. I thought Dad's Weekend at my college was a holiday in my honor.

Brooklyn's mom and I were quickly married and genially divorced and afterward we raised Brooklyn in an experiment marked by good intentions and modest communication. Even in the best divorce, every detail of parenting must be negotiated. Bedtime is the Middle East Peace Accords, curfew the Geneva Conventions. It was in this spirit that we set out to map our daughter's religious upbringing.

Brooklyn's mother was a Catholic who, early on, wanted Brooklyn to attend parochial school and be confirmed in the Catholic religion. I agreed, in part because I didn't have an alternative (there being so few Jainist elementary schools in America). But as parents we also want our kids to have access to everything—those things we had and those that we didn't. So I wanted Brooklyn to be a star athlete, to go to an Ivy League college, and to have faith in... *something.* The last thing I wanted was for her to be saddled with her father's bad eyesight, his procrastination, or his aching doubt that the world has meaning. The last thing I wanted was for her to lie in bed having nightmares about hell. So my parenting plan was simple: downplay my agnosticism, at least for a while. Let Brooklyn's mother handle the spiritual side of childrearing.

Of course, a parent can't withhold his belief system anymore than he can withhold his hair color. And the trouble begins as soon as the little buggers start to talk. I can still see Brooklyn in the rearview mirror, straining in her car seat to see something and then turning forward to ask me, "Daddy, why are trees green?"

This is the crux of the problem: How does the well-meaning agnostic remain truthful to his own beliefs while still passing on to his children some sense of spiritual stability, some warm blanket of faith, some way to measure the mystical and the lovely?

"Well, honey. There's this thing called photosynthesis, in which ... uh ... sunlight activates ... uh ... chlorophyll ... and, um ... carbon dioxide—"

"No, Daddy. Who *made* them green?"

It turns out that I do have a kind of faith. I have faith in the power of a good story. I have faith in the grace of a hopeful lie.

"Well, honey . . . I suppose . . . God did. God made the trees green."

I tend to marry Catholics.

Seventeen years after Cookie Church incident, and nine years after my first wedding, I was to be married again in the Catholic Church. My wonderful fiancée, Anne, had always wanted to be wed in her family's parish church, and the priest informed us that we could do this as long as I'd been baptized in some form of Christian faith.

This was no problem. After all, I was saved.

We called my mom and she said she'd look for my baptismal

certificate. But a week before the wedding she still hadn't found it and the priest was getting impatient. I volunteered to help look through boxes in the garage. Or maybe, I said, we could call the church where I'd been christened to see if they had records. That's when my mom burst into tears. "Oh Jess. I'm so sorry. There *is* no certificate. You were never baptized."

It was quiet for a minute. The only sound in the room was my mother's crying.

Apparently, after Cookie Church, I had been so inconsolable she told me that I was baptized just to get me to stop crying. Now my mom was inconsolable. She told me she felt awful for lying to me. Finally, I took her hand and told her it was fine. "You know what, Mom? It's okay. I don't even *believe* in that crap."

This did not seem to make her feel better.

My mom died of cancer a few years later. She was only 53. It was unbearably sad and unfair. She was the best person I knew. To my knowledge, my baptism was the only thing she ever lied about. In the weeks before her death she talked courageously about her life and its end. She had few regrets. Among the biggest, she said, was that she hadn't given my brother and sister and me a Christian upbringing. She herself had always had a quiet faith and she felt badly that her kids didn't seem to share it. In her last days, she asked to see a nondenominational minister, who baptized her. When it was done she looked around for a while, then lay back and went to sleep. I sat by her bed all night, as she had the night I had nightmares of hell. I watched closely, trying to feel some change in the room, some spiritual presence. There was nothing but her ragged breathing and the grinding of her morphine pump.

There are a million things I wish I could tell my mother now. I would tell her about her grandchildren, how they got her warmth and creativity and her long skinny fingers. I would tell her that not a day goes by that I don't think about her. And I would tell her this:

Mom. I never felt more profoundly loved than the day I found out you lied about my being saved.

Parenthood makes sweet hypocrites of us all.

I know strict vegetarians whose kids eat only hot dogs. I have seen people decry the insidious power of television, then turn their children over to SpongeBob so they can have five minutes of peace, so they can take a *freaking shower*. I myself am a strident believer in the public school system who drops his kids off at private school every morning.

This is one of the great things about children. Orthodoxy crumbles in their presence. Every parent is a little bit agnostic; every parent is a grudging relativist.

My first child, Brooklyn, is nineteen now, smart and beautiful, cutting her own path as a seeker and a skeptic. When she was old enough, we talked about the hypocrisy of organized religion, and about my agnosticism. Brooklyn likes yoga now and books about Eastern religions. She no longer attends Catholic Church. Maybe its only purpose was to give her a frame of reference, something to rebel against, like kicking off the wall of a swimming pool. And maybe, like a swimming pool wall, it will be there one day if she's afraid of drowning. Either way, I think it will have been a positive force in her life.

So, too, will her dad's loose sect of the storyteller.

Brooklyn struggled with my mom's death, in part, I see now, because I tried to shield her from its pain. A few years earlier, her mother's best friend died of leukemia, days before she was supposed to get married. Brooklyn's view of the world has always included the bullying capriciousness of cancer.

When she was fourteen Brooklyn wrote a short story about two girls, best friends who pass notes back and forth beneath their desks every day in elementary school, and who are nervously about to enter the mysterious world of middle school together. Then one of the girls becomes sick. The whole story is self-contained in a single day, a journey in which the healthy girl, Allison, tries to see her friend at the hospital. She waits at a bus stop, then rides the bus, and finally arrives at the hospital, where teary-eyed adults won't meet her eyes. Ultimately, Allison isn't allowed to see her friend. She is sent home with a box from her sick friend. At home, Allison opens the box. Inside is a picture of the two girls and one last note passed beneath the eyes of adults. The note says that the dying girl will miss her friend, and that she wishes they could go to middle school together. And that's it. Maybe the best thing we can do for one another is to say good-bye.

Sometimes, when I'm torturing the keys of my computer, I wonder if I'll ever write anything as perfect as that little story.

My wife has a bedrock and reasonable faith. I used to try engaging her in chess-game debates over the hypocrisies of Catholicism. But Anne laughed at my belligerence and said that her faith wasn't contained in any doctrine or church, certainly not in any old bishop or any building in Rome. She goes to Catholic Church not because she believes every part of it, but because that's where she was raised, and that's where she feels close to God. She doesn't ask God what he looks like, or for his views on stem cell research. She just allows him to be. At her church, she finds a community of people looking beyond their jobs and their houses, coming together to contemplate the inscrutable nature of their spiritual selves.

My rebuttal went something like this: Oh.

It was like someone holding up a blooming flower and saying, Debate this.

Anne and I have two earnest and brilliant kids. Ava is seven. Alec is four. They go to Catholic school and church, and I have seen in them the very quality that I love and envy in Anne. *Belief.* I try to encourage this; the other day, when Alec asked me who made trees, I only hesitated a moment: "God did." I can explain photosynthesis and Jainism later.

I'm grateful to Anne that my children have her faith. But I am glad, too, that they are steeped, like their older sister, Brooklyn, in their dad's belief in the story, in the power and grace of the artful lie. Ava is a voracious reader who has been writing "books" for as long as she could talk, at first dictating the stories to me and now writing and illustrating them herself. Ava's latest was called *The Princess and the Hippie*, about a princess who objects to a "hippie beggar girl" who is always panhandling outside the castle gate. The story climaxes with a sword battle during which the protagonist reveals herself to be a hippie-beggar-*warrior*, who then drives away the palace guards, befriends the Princess, and goes with her to the beach.

Alec, too, has begun writing stories. The first one was dictated to me and illustrated by him on a napkin at a restaurant. It appears with the permission of the author who, after a bitter negotiation, sold its one-time rights to me a few minutes ago for a handful of trail mix and a juice box:

"The fire was burning. Soon, it went right over the kids. And then it burned the slide. And then what happened, the slide went down in one big pile. The Great Wall of China was up. Soon a fire lit up. The fire got the Great Wall of China. Soon it was just one big pile."

Amen.

So I've been thinking lately about getting baptized. I'm not sure why, exactly. But that's the great thing about being agnostic. You don't have to know why. In fact, you *can't* know why.

Maybe I'll wait until I'm near death, then summon a pastor the way my mom did. Maybe I'll do it sooner. Maybe I won't do it at all. Will it have value if, in the end, I can't convince myself it's anything more than a few drops of water dribbled on my head? Will I even find a priest or a minister willing to baptize someone who plans to give nothing in return: no commitment, no pledge to believe, no promises to follow rules or tithe or vote a certain way?

I don't know. But frankly, I'm not above a provisional move like this. If there's a chance that my family is going somewhere after this life, I'll dine on a little hypocrisy to try to go with them. And if I can, I'll tell the pastor so: Look, I don't really believe in this. But I want to be baptized for my wife and my kids.

I want to be baptized for my mom.

But there's another part that appeals to me: the narrative symmetry of it. The agnostic's baptism satisfies my writer's sensibility. It seems to me the perfect ending, hopeful but not overly sentimental, nicely symbolic but suitably open-ended, touched by blessed ambiguity.

In my mind, the story ends with the skeptic allowing the drops to run down his forehead, two cool paths to his eyes. Then he falls back into bed and looks around at the faces of his family, closes his eyes and wishes once more that he believed in something, so he could offer this prayer: Thank you—Whoever You Are, or Aren't—for the gift of these people, for my parents and my brother and sister, for my children and my wife, these people who gave my life meaning, these people for whom I choose to irrationally douse my head in water, these people in whose love I was redeemed, and—Oh, what the hell, you never know—saved.

Laura Read

Emmanuel

Ordinarily, I love Advent, the Christian season of waiting in darkness for a great light. I love the dark church, the cold pews, the flickering candles in the wreath, the smell of pine, and the song "O Come, O Come Emmanuel" rising from the base of my stomach like the light rising from the long wick, a desire, a plea, spreading through the church like light, and later, smoke. But the year I was pregnant with Matthew, Advent was a month not of expectation but fear; my prayers flew toward the candles, purple, purple, pink, purple, and then finally white, with increasing desperation. Each week, my stomach growing larger on my lap, I waited for my great light, the verdict I so hoped the ultrasound that January would deliver: *It's a girl*. But each Sunday, the darkness inside of me grew deeper as I realized that I actually feared the other possibility, that it would be another boy. I felt this fear and the shame of having it: what kind of mother would not just be grateful for a healthy baby? Wasn't my first son, Benjamin, already everything I could want in a child? What difference would a daughter make? This was the question that always stopped me in my self-punishment. For even though I was raised by a feminist sociologist, I still believed that a daughter would make a difference, a difference I needed. And so, as Christmas approached, came, and passed, I prayed—in the church, in the living room, in the kitchen, looking out at the snow falling and falling—for my girl.

I remember the date of the ultrasound: January 11, 2002. I was nervous all day. When the technician began moving the wand over my stomach, it was like I already knew. During Benjamin's ultrasound, we thought we were getting good at figuring out the images but then wrongly identified his hand as his heart, but this time, right away, Matthew's bones seemed to make sense to me, lit up like stars across a plane of night, a constellation of joints and white light. The doctor went slowly, checking the brain and heart carefully, and there was a healthy part of me that was just praying for a healthy baby, but the other part, dark and persistent, had already seen a penis, was sure, but was also dying for the doctor to say no, that's her arm. The time moved excruciatingly slowly, but finally he asked if we wanted to know the sex, and we said yes. There was no air in my lungs. He pointed to what I'd seen and said, *There. It's a boy.* We asked if he was positive, and he grinned and said 100 percent. Inside me, I felt like I was falling down a long tunnel, like Alice in Wonderland.

Of course, there were other moments during the ultrasound that peeked through like slices of sun through a thick forest. At one point, Matthew turned and I could see his whole face, and it was beautiful. It was like he looked right at me. I saw his thumb in his mouth. I saw hair on the top of his head. And there was a moment of genuine worry when the technician went to get the doctor to check something in the heart. For that minute, the girl washed away like a dream disintegrated by the clamor of an alarm clock, but when the doctor reassured us, I filled up again with my familiar, inexplicable sorrow.

Benjamin was at my mother's house. I cried the whole way there, my hands resting on the healthy boy growing inside me. When she opened the door, it was like she had also already known; right away she asked, *Is he healthy?* She was jubilant, trying to sweep me up with her into the appropriate feeling. I hugged Benjamin, but I was like a clock with one of my complicated brass pieces not turning correctly with the others. Time moved, but I did not keep up with it. My husband, Brad, only wanted to have two children, and here they were, sons. I was the oldest in my family of five, the only girl, one brother following another, and now the march of boys continued. At dinner, my mother joked that we had been given a mission, to raise fine men, which the world badly needed. I tried to laugh. After dinner, we showed the videotape of the ultrasound to my mother and Benjamin. *There's your brother*, we said.

That night, after Ben was asleep, I hemmed my maternity pajamas, studying the teacups and teapots in the pattern, and I thought about girls. I loved those pajamas; they were so girl-y, like me. I like tea parties and *Madeline* and *Anne of Green Gables* and *Little Women*. I like patchwork and ringlets and dresses with birds and flowers and strawberries on them. I like to stay inside, rain or shine, and read and dress up and bake and talk. I like home. There are pictures of me as a child in seersucker summer outfits with fruit on them and matching bonnets, and in fall and winter in corduroy dresses and my Irish sweater and matching hat. I was chubby, and I even had chubby hair, big fat red curls, and big brown eyes. I envisioned that my daughter would look just like that little girl. Once, looking at baby clothes, I felt my chest throb when I touched a little girl dress with a lace collar that reminded me of my girl, the one in my mind, the one I had always kept with me. When I took a nap alone, I pretended she lay next to me, my arm covering her, rising and falling with her breath. There she was, red curls, a little chubby, wearing new versions of my old clothes, and when she woke up, she smiled at me, small mirrors in her eyes.

I never liked boys. I liked my brothers and my fathers (after my first father died, my mom remarried). I liked my husband. But the whole idea of *boy* I detested. I don't like video games or sports, aggression or anger, or even adventure really. I was already raising my boy much like a girl, hopefully not to his detriment. We had tea parties and read both girl and boy books and did art and baked and talked a lot. I felt very close to him, but I feared that would change as he grew up. My brothers had, one by one, grown distant from my mother. They have to be drawn out. They have to be implored to stay in. They have to be endlessly fed and picked up after. And I was always my mother's companion, leaning on the kitchen counter telling her about school, cutting vegetables for the salad, giving my brothers their baths. Who would be my companion? To whom would I pass down heirlooms—my grandmother's prayerbook, her locket, her platter? Who would I have to identify with me, because even if we shared little else, like I sometimes feel is true about my own mother and me, we would at least both be women.

Of course, I realize how my views on gender are based on stereotypes, and I don't often admit to actually holding them. In fact, while I hold them, I also hold their opposite, believing that gender is a social construct not a biological dictate, just as I've been taught. But as my contradictions illustrate, I've been taught one idea in words and the other in action, creating confusion and an ache that has persisted in me through the rest of my second pregnancy and through Matthew's first two years of life.

I thought when I saw Matthew, when he turned toward me as he had in the ultrasound, the dream of the girl would vanish completely, but I still woke at night with the feeling there was something bad sleep had made me forget, something about to come back to me, and then it whispered, *You don't have her. You'll never have your girl.* Even when I looked over at him, sleeping in his crib or curled next to me in the bed, though I was always broken open by the beauty of his face, carved into marble in sleep, his sweet breath blowing in and out, his cheeks full and his hair filling in like a field in spring, my satisfaction was not the complete feeling I'd had in my dream with her beside me or the feeling I'd had with Benjamin when I knew she was still possible. The shame was still there, the shame of failing to love my son that completely, of still longing for her. I started to think maybe the ache wasn't going to go away.

I remembered that shame from the beginning of my marriage, and it still played in the background here and there, like an old song on the radio containing an old feeling. My love for Brad was bordered by the other loves that had gone before him, perfected by loss, and by the love I'd spent my childhood dreaming up. I loved him, but I wondered about the other lives I would never have, the ones I'd revoked by choosing this one man with his one body, tall and broad-chested, the smell of Old Spice in his shirts, his anger at injustice burning like embers, quiet and hot. I loved how he loved me, how he listened and understood, but I also wanted a movie star, a man of few words who would come and go as he liked, always leaving me hanging and breathless with mystery. I also remembered the same feeling from childhood, never being fully happy in the present moment, with what I had. My mother used to tell me, in moments of frustration, that I was bottomless. I was confused when she told me this because I really thought there was a bottom, something that would fill me up.

From as far back as I can remember, I wanted that something. Perhaps it even began before my father died, but I remember well the year after his death, when I was six. That was when I started to have insomnia. When my mother put me to bed at night, she would sit down next to me for a few minutes, and I would beg her to stay. I felt bad about the loneliness and desperation I felt, but I just had to have her. When she left, I tried to be brave, knowing I was skating on the edge of her patience. I would focus on the tiny light of my nightlight and then the large stuffed camel on my floor. I held my panda bear tight or made him do gymnastics on my chest. I stared at the picture, made of felt on canvas, of a blonde woman standing under an apple tree. The woman looked like my mother. Next to it, there was a picture from my first communion of a child resting in the hand of God. I closed my eyes and tried to imagine myself in God's hand, and His hand became my father's hand, and as they blended, sometimes I fell asleep.

In the day, I comforted myself by keeping a constant din of counting and listing going in my mind. I had to work hard at not feeling sad, at not being afraid all the time, and at trying not to be myself. I grew up feeling like all the traits I had were the wrong ones. I was introverted in an extroverted culture, chubby in a thin culture, girlie in a masculine culture. I was not assertive, competitive, or athletic. I wanted to fit in, so in high school I valiantly tried to do so. I became a cheerleader, I made lots of friends, I was in all the plays and musicals (even though I couldn't sing), and I even went to parties, although beer and boys both terrified me. I went to college in my hometown, to be close to my mother, but she was disappointed in me for not being more adventurous. So I went to Paris for a junior year abroad to please her, and there I was finally left completely alone with my mind. In a way, this is what I thought I'd always wanted. I never liked to reach my destination when I was driving in a car because I liked having the time alone to figure out my own thoughts. I never felt that I could be myself with other people. So you'd think it would have been a relief to be alone with just a handful of Americans in a sea of French. But instead, it was worse. I guess I knew that underneath the din I'd created, there was something I felt was bad, so in France, I just made the din louder. I wrote long lists over and over again; I ran constant small, unnecessary errands. I went sightseeing with great deliberation and care; I spent hours at night recording my every move and thought in letters to home. If I left a feeling or thought unshared, it frightened me. And I began to understand that being alone was the very thing I most feared.

After Matthew, even though I was surrounded by people, I felt the Paris feelings coming back, and once again, I was afraid of feeling them by myself, so I went to a counselor. Of course, I thought she was irritating: She would not tell me who I was, what was wrong with me, or give me any solutions. She asked me questions and waited. I thought, *I could do this at home.* But one question did interrupt the hamster wheel in my brain for a minute. Why did I need a daughter? And then other questions: Why a different husband? Or my father? Without these things, what was the worst thing that could happen? And why was I so afraid to be alone? I knew the answer right away. Or rather, I pictured it.

My mother sits alone in her living room. It's one in the morning, and she's still awake, reading and smoking. Only one light is on, no music. Upstairs, my dad is sleeping, but all the kids are grown now, sleeping far away, and she feels their absence behind every closed door, in every made bed. She brings the cigarette to her lip and breathes it in, the flame crinkling at the tip, a gesture I've always envied, the grace of her arm moving through the air, the cigarette held skillfully between her fingers, the ability of the body to bring itself relief, to breathe in a feeling to cover another one.

On her calendar, she lists all her things to do in the box of each day and puts a checkmark beside each one when it's completed. When I was a child, the oldest of five, each day was crowded, full of work and doctor appointments, school commitments, household chores. Different colors of ink gave the page of each month a look of chaos, and our life matched the calendar. My mom's checkmarks brought some order, as did her time in the chair at the end of the day. But now on her calendar, she writes bigger to fill up the boxes. She has to walk the dog, go to the gym, and on Thursday this week, she'll have coffee with a student. She still checks things off even though there's so much less to remember, so much less to control.

My dad works a lot, twelve-hour shifts, so sometimes she'll go for days with just her own company, company she missed when the kids were little, like she misses the kids now. But at least she has me. I didn't leave for college, and after Paris, I came back. I will probably never leave her. I spent my childhood following her around while she dusted, sent a sheet billowing out over a bed, folded little boys' clothes. When my first dad died and she couldn't get out of the green chair, I made macaroni. When she had her hysterectomy, I scrubbed the kitchen floor on my hands and knees. I tried so hard to be just like her, so it has taken me years to realize we're not alike. But I love her with the fierce, unthinking loyalty of a dog, and as a dog senses her owner's spirits and sits closer, I know that on the inside we are made of the same fear, big like the ocean, and seemingly bottomless.

So when the counselor asks me what is the worst thing that could happen, I say that I will be like my mother. That I will lose my husband like she did. That I will not have the companionship I need. That my kids will grow up and leave me. That I will sit alone at night in my pool of lamplight, reading novel after novel, trying to pour words over my words, without even the comfort of smoke, or my grandmother's medicine, scotch. I see the chicken bones of my grandmother's ankles shaking as she sat up late, reading romances, mourning the loss of her own. But here's the important thing, I tell my counselor, the difference. My grandmother, Cecilia, had Jane. And Jane has me. But I don't have a daughter. Who will be my Laura?

Of course, the counselor reminds me that my husband has not died. But that is not the point. He will die. Men don't last; daughters do. I know this is irrational, but there it is anyway. No one will be there to save me from the emptiness. When I picture death, I see myself splayed across the heavens, cold blackness all around me, and everyone I love is there, but they are far away. I can see them, but I will never touch them again. I will be all alone in space. My counselor proposes other images, but I don't listen. She says things that embarrass me, cheesy metaphors that counselors use. She says maybe *I* can be my Laura. She says maybe the imaginary little girl sleeping next to me in my bed is not just like me; maybe she is me. I think, *maybe*, but how will just me ever be enough? I am still afraid to be left alone with my own mind, with its compulsions, its repetitions, all its little trapdoors. Like my body, it is difficult to love. I still feel like there is something wrong with me, something missing that everyone else has.

For a long time, I hated our old house just because it wasn't a new house. I didn't focus on its character and charms, its carpentry and wainscoting, but rather on all its creaks and leaks. Lately, I've begun to love it, eagerly lavishing it with new rugs and towels, lovingly wiping dust from its surfaces. But then I found out that one side of its foundation is sinking into the ground. We're tilted and, like the *Titanic*, we're going down. And sadly, the analogy still works. I feel like even if I can love some parts of me, even if there could be some happiness, sitting alone in my chair in my old age there would still be that flaw in the foundation, some spiritual crack I'll fall through into space.

So, I think, if my counselor were here, this is when she would ask another one of her questions. *And what would be the worst thing about that?* And she would answer for me, *Sure, it's cold, but it's also lovely. And it won't just be you. God will be with you.*

God will be with you. The promise of Emmanuel, the meaning of his name, the song we sing every Advent, *oh come again, God, be with us.* Though it was a comfort to me in childhood, often, as an adult, my faith in God is not strong. My husband is not religious, and, in part because of his influence, I have moved away from church. But this past Sunday, I did go to church, and I remembered one of the things I most love about it: when the readings seem to speak to you directly, like sometimes your horoscope does, tricking you into believing the stars do govern your life. Is my Christianity a trick? Whenever I asked my mother about doubting God, she told me that in the Narnia stories when someone challenges Puddleglum's faith in Narnia, he says that he'd rather live his life believing in it than not. On Sunday, this is just how I felt when I listened to the lector read Psalm 139, a reading I'd heard many times before: "O Lord, you have searched me and known me…. For it was you who formed my inward parts; you knit me together in my mother's womb…. How weighty to me are your thoughts, O God! How vast is the sum of them! I try to count them—they are more than the sand; I come to the end—I am still with you" (verses 1, 13, 17–18).

In the beginning, God was there, and in the end, He will still be there. He (or She) has always been there, I guess, underneath the din, with the pain. I love the image of knitting the child together, of knowing the secret making in the womb, all the details of a person, good and bad, and loving all of it. When I go into my sons' room at night and watch them sleep, I understand this a little. It is a different closeness we share then than the one we feel in the day. I rub their hair like I did in their infancy, pressing it softly against their heads. I know each freckle on their bodies. I arrange their blankets even though I know they'll kick them off again. I think about all the ways they challenge me and all the ways they fill me with joy, and I love seeing them like this, in the gray quiet of their room, humidifier whirring comfortingly, their artwork on the walls, clouds on their sheets. In these moments, I love them wholly, and I imagine this is the kind of love God feels for us.

When I was a child, my mother said I should pray to my father. Probably she thought it would be easier for me to picture God through someone I'd known. She was right. God still looks like Richard to me, dark hair and olive skin, skinny, a good dancer. Or rather he looks like the photographs of Richard, the few video images with Creedence Clearwater Revival playing in the background, since my real memories of him are confused. And my mother and I joke about Richard looking down on us; she says she can't think he's always looking, or she would never go to the bathroom! But still, she thinks she feels him when a certain song comes on the radio, and I think I feel him when I pray. So, in the end, he will be with me as well.

It's getting better. When I think of my mom alone at night or of my childhood bedroom, I still feel afraid. But I try to stay in the rooms a bit and pray. When I think of not having a daughter like me, I think at least I have me, and that's not bad. And I have Benjamin and Matthew.

Matthew. On the days I believe in an interfering sort of God, not the clockmaker but the one with the plan for my life, I believe he sent me Matthew on purpose, laughing at his own mischief. Benjamin has big eyes with dark lashes and a full head of curly hair; when he was a baby, people often mistook him for a girl. But once, in a department store, a woman looked at Matthew and said, "Now that one is all boy." And he is. Since the beginning, he has loved trucks and sticks, just as people say boys do, without any encouragement from me. He's built like a little football player, and since my husband's nickname was Stubby when he was little, we sometimes call Matthew Stubby Jr. He loves sports, and he always wants to wrestle. Also, he has quite a temper. He is sweet and loving one minute and then screaming mad the next. In contrast, I see how much Benjamin is like me, perhaps even more than a daughter would be: quieter than his brother, prone to melancholy not anger, dramatic, a bookworm, an artist. But it is not as simple as this, of course. Matthew is also like me: silly, sweet, sleepy, devoted, a homebody. So it's as if God said, *You want a girl? You think you need her?* You don't. Here's Benjamin. Here's Matthew. Here's you.

Here's you. All spiritual lessons seem to me to be clichés dressed up in new clothes. A child is fulfilling, but he is not your fulfillment. Without my two sons, I'm not sure I would have found my emptiness. I so much wanted a daughter, a little me I could protect and fill with safety and warmth, a little me who would later keep me warm and safe. But I didn't get her, and if I had, we couldn't have kept each other safe from loss; she would have had her own emptiness to face, as I still have mine. I always remember a line from a novel I read shortly after Matt was born, Whitney Otto's *A Collection of Beauties at the Height of Their Popularity*, which reads: "I discovered that you can refuse something and still it stays with you." This stays with me, for even as I write this, I realize I am trying to settle something that won't be settled, trying to play the last song and roll the credits.

After my dad died, "If You Leave Me Now" by Chicago seemed like it was always playing on the radio (it was 1977). Riding in the car with my mother and brother, I would look out the window, sometimes at the rain and sometimes pretending it was raining, and imagine someone looking in, the water streaking the glass and giving the appearance of tears on my face, as I looked soulfully out at the streets and houses we passed. When the song ended, or when we arrived wherever we were going, I was always a little amazed when my mom cut the engine and got out of the car. The movie was never over. The pain never completely heals and the lesson is never fully learned. That must be why it bears repeating.

In my movie now, the stars are men: large and small. And I am close to each of them, because of our similarities and our differences. But nothing undoes the loss of my imaginary daughter, the loss of my real father, or the great fear I still have of change and loss. But by not being what I always wanted, my sons have been what I always wanted. The hours I've spent rocking them, their bodies folded into mine, has helped heal me, and the pain I've felt because of them has oddly done the same. When our movie is over, when it is a movie with its own music playing in the background, its few images repeating, one Christmas caught perhaps, one night of dancing in the living room in pajamas, I hope they will feel that the pain and the love I will have passed on to them has helped them better understand this life, and I hope they also believe that God, and I, will always be with them.

2:45 P.M.

In school portraits tacked over my desk, you can see them at seven and five: Captain America and his little brother, the Refugee. Hayes makes a smirky Captain in his blue Cub Scout uniform and shiny helmet of hair, arms folded statesmanlike on the desk before him. Poor Vincent could qualify for social services on the basis of this photograph alone, I fear, eyelids half-mast, face covered with boo-boos, one ear blending with some books on a shelf in the background so that it looks outsized and deformed, like a leaf of a radicchio.

How is it that these school mug shots can turn the most photogenic little angel into a sickly goon who seems to be smiling despite the matchsticks wedged under his fingernails? And the prices! I'll take the Bargain Bonanza Package for forty-five bucks, please. Couldn't pass up those two dozen bonus wallets.

"Dear Mom," says an old Mother's Day letter posted beside the photos, written in shaky, fresh-minted cursive handwriting on a blue-lined paper. "I really like when you take me to the movies. You are special because you cook what I like. I want to help you clean the house. I really like how you smile. I have a surprise for you. Love, Hayes."

He wanted to help me clean the house? That was surprise enough. Another missive is penciled on a bunny cut out from yellow construction paper: "Dear Mom. I love you Mom. Happy

Spring Break Mom. When can Will come over."

Vincie, who doesn't write letters yet, is represented by artwork: a penciled depiction of a martian and his pet shark, living in a castle full of fax machines and Nintendo controllers; another sheet printed all over with a rubber stamp of Vincent Winik's return address, some wobbly pink hearts, two figures with big smiles and bifurcated flippers for arms, and one word: MOM.

Some days—like maybe three out of a hundred—I am just so busy riding a tsunami of productivity in this home office of mine, I wish I didn't have to drop everything at 2:40 in the afternoon to go pick up my little pals at school. Far more likely, I start checking the clock at eleven, if not before, and count the minutes until it's time to go. Not only because it means I get to escape the solitude of the so-called creative process for a few hours and resume my role as household drudge, math tutor, and nuthouse warden, but also because I can't wait to see them, to repossess them, to get them back on my territory, whole, healthy and breathing—in part, the same impulse that used to drive me to check their baby cribs midnap. Of course, this feeling of anticipation involves a bit of willful tip-toeing around the possibility of an Awful Afternoon with the Devil Brats from Hell, but hey, why not be optimistic.

I fly out the door and into the Jeep and have to force myself to slow down to twenty miles per hour as I reach the speed bumps and blinking lights of SCHOOL ZONE. I pull into the circular drive of the brick elementary school behind the minivans and Volvos and pickup trucks, and my personal favorite, the flower-power-printed Volkswagen Beetle that belongs to a local family doctor, reportedly equipped with a car phone but no air conditioning.

On the bench under a live oak tree, a mom with a Keith Haring button and black leggings is chatting amiably with a dad in a three-piece suit. Baby brothers and sisters mill around as their mothers stand in clusters, deconstructing last night's PTA meeting with the earnestness of Harvard graduate students, and representatives from various after-school programs stand ready with clipboards to gather up their broods. I spy the fund-raising coordinator and wander over to find out when I'm scheduled to sell grocery certificates but am waylaid en route by the soccer coach and the plant sale chairwoman. BRYKER WOODS ELEMENTARY, says my mental bumper sticker for this place, WHERE PARENT INVOLVEMENT IS A SICKNESS.

The hair-raisingly loud buzzer euphemistically known as the "bell" goes off, the blue-green doors fly open, and the kids start tumbling out: the kindergarteners with their toystore backpacks and Velcroed sneakers, who already look so tiny to me; the unimaginably grown-up sixth-graders, with skateboards and cellos and streaks of orange dyed into their hair; and all the many kids from grades in between who wear the same haircut as my kids do, so that almost daily, at least for a fraction of a second, I mistake someone else for mine.

And I'm still searching the crowd when one of them skids up in front of me: my first-grader, Vince, his six-and-a-half-year-old body coltlike, skinny and knobby under the baggy, faded, torn-up, mismatched clothes he would rather die for than throw away. Though he seems to get taller almost daily and can prepare a can of chicken noodle soup from start to finish without assistance, his face still wears the heart-tuggingly pure expression of one who has not completed the transition from baby to boy: something in his round blue eyes and jutting pink lower lip is as radiantly unformed, as clear and open, as it was when he was an infant waking up in his bassinet. He refuses to tie his shoes or get out of bed in the mornings, he has a wide lazy streak, a thirst for sibling combat, a madman's scream, and a whine that could probably serve as a form of torture in a pinch, but you can still see the other-worldly sweetness that he came with from the factory, which had his father and me insisting half-seriously to our acquaintances that we had given birth to the Baby Messiah.

"Can Calvin come home with me?" the former baby messiah wants to know. "Please, Mom, please, he really wants to."

"Well, I'd really love him to, too, but you know we have to make plans with his mom the night before we want to have him over."

"I *never* get to have anyone over!" says Vince, resorting to his favorite negotiation strategy, what surely must be chapter one in the six-year-olds' edition of *The Art of the Deal*. "You *always* say no! You never let me do anything!" he folds his arms and pushes his lower lip as far out as it will go, a key element of this diplomatic technique.

"Vincie, there's nothing I can do about it. If we don't make advance arrangements so his mom can send a note, she gets fined by the whatchamacallit place he's supposed to go."

"All right," he exhales grumpily, and turns to go report the bad news to Calvin. The first three steps are an exaggerated shuffle of despair, then he lapses back into the usual skip. When he returns, I am gazing at him with a goofy smile of adoration.

"How come you look so happy today?" he asks me suspiciously. He asks me this almost every day.

"You know why," I say.

"Because you're so happy to see me?"

"Yup," I say, "that's why." And then he looks at me with an expression that is half pleased, half embarrassed ("That Mom. She's a moron, but she's *our* moron") and gives me a quick hug. Just because I still can, I grab him, whoosh him in the air, and bounce him over to the car, and he's grinning from the sheer fun of being tossed around.

"Okay," I say, "where's your brother?" I visually pick through the jumble of kids turning somersaults on the bike rack, others tossing a football on the lawn.

"Mommy," says Vince—who is a chatterbox given to long, often confusing monologues, and something about this "Mommy" seems to herald one—"guess what happened? Frederick got sent to the North Pole because he wouldn't stop talking during story and all the other boys got in trouble too butcept me and Mrs. Harverstick came and gave me a sticker and—"

It kills me when he says "butcept." But I must interrupt.

"Vincie, go get Hayes," I order, spotting his brother engaged in some important third-grade powwow with two friends. "See him back there by the fence?"

"But don't you want to see my sticker?"

"Of course I do, sweetie. Oh, wow! That's great! Now go get Hayes."

"Hayes!" Vincie bellows without moving an inch.

Hayes, whose ears have somehow picked up the brother frequency over the din of the schoolyard, says good-bye to his friends and comes toward us. He's wearing his blue-and-white Dallas Cowboys jersey, matching navy shorts, and pair of over-sized white high-tops that are endorsed by, and indeed almost look as if they would fit, Hakeem Olajuwon. His hair still shows a trace of the spray gel I was begged to comb in this morning to make it stay over to the side like that of a currently idolized classmate. Unlike his little brother, Hayes at nine is all the way to boy, and sometimes beyond: his handsome, longish face already wears the ironic expression that his father's did, amusement play-ing around the mouth, but a seriousness, a certain concern, in the warm brown eyes.

"Hey, Mom," he says, his eyes on a cluster of friends rough-housing nearby. He reaches to tweak the backpack strap of a pass-ing buddy.

"How was school today?"

"Great," says Hayes. That's what he always says. That's what they all say. The public schools could be teaching guerrilla tac-tics, animal husbandry, or Sanskrit grammar all day and the par-ents of America would be the last to know.

"Can you be more specific? Did anything interesting happen? If I'm not going to get a hug, could we at least make eye con-tact?"

He gives me a grin and a quick hug. Score! But wait, there's more: "Mom, can we stop and get a Slim Jim or something? I'm starving half to death!"

"Me, too," Vincie chimes in at his elbow, looking to see if Brother Boss Man has noted his helpful contribution to the hun-ger relief effort.

"Get in the car and put on your seat belts," I command.

"But Mom, it was Sloppy Joes for lunch and it was so gross I couldn't even eat it."

"All right, all right! We'll stop at the store! Now come on, let's get going. How much homework do you have? Hey! Stop playing with that ball in the car! I can't drive! Put it away! Do you want to go to the store? Then put the ball in the back seat! Now!"

No one is paying any attention to me at all. Well, I'm used to it. I reach one arm back, knock the ball away, start the car, and ease out into traffic. The afternoon sun is in my eyes, but I can't find my sunglasses in the heap of army men, half-melted crayons, and cassette boxes beside me. The boys are punching each other; Hayes is singing "Nacho Nacho Nacho Man, I want to be a Nacho Man" over and over in a monotone; Vincie's backpack is full of gravel and dirt, which he's dumping out on the seat of the car; and we're on our way to the grocery store to get Slim Jims and a box of macaroni.

I'm with my boys, and all is right with the world.

Rosemary Bray McNatt

Birthing a New World

Every Mother's Day I wear a red carnation. People don't wear Mother's Day carnations as much as they used to, but I always try to wear a real carnation, because where I grew up, that was a Mother's Day tradition. The selling of Mother's Day carnations, in fact, was a kind of two-day cottage industry on the South Side of Chicago.

The color of a Mother's Day carnation matters. A red carnation means your mother is alive. A white carnation means your mother has died. I turned fifty this year. All these years, I've been able to wear a red carnation on Mother's Day. For that same number of years—for all of her conscious life, in fact, my mother has always worn a white carnation, because her mother (my grandmother) died when she was only two years old.

When I was little, there were two things I always wondered about on Mother's Day: I wondered how Mama must feel to be the only one among us who wore a white flower. And I wondered and feared what it would be like when Mama died and it was my turn to wear a white carnation. But I figured I'd grow out of it, because grownups, I reasoned, were big enough not to wonder or be afraid. So now I'm grown up, and there are three things I always wonder about on Mother's Day. I wonder how Mama feels to pick up her white flower for another year. I wonder, and fear, what life will be like when my mother is gone, when it is my turn to wear a white carnation. And now, as a mother, I wonder what it will be like for my sons when I am gone, when it is their turn to wear white.

Several years ago, after starting seminary, I attended a denominational meeting at which an old friend was present. He's been a minister for a long time, and we've served on a couple of committees together. We hadn't seen each other for a long time, so he and I broke away from the group for lunch. As we ate and talked, we reflected on all the years we'd known each other, and how for much of that time, I was a laywoman who talked a lot about staying a laywoman. I mentioned how weird it was to think back on those times, and to find myself now, neck deep in both motherhood and seminary. I may have mentioned somewhere in the conversation that clearly I was crazy to be doing all this stuff at once, and wondered, not for the first time, how it was that I'd decided on the ministry now, perhaps at the most inconvenient possible time in my whole life. My friend was quick to answer: "Oh, that's easy. It was having the children," he told me. "That's what broke your heart open."

What broke my heart open, I thought. What a funny thing to say. And yet the more I thought of it, the more the truth of it became clear. I always cared about life, about things, about people —but in a distant, nearly theoretical way. Joining every committee and working group that presented itself was something I had been doing for years. For part of that time, I thought I might have experienced the call to ordained ministry. But it was a thought I dismissed over and over again. Ministers had to be different, better than the rest of us. I could never do what was required; the depth and breadth and seriousness of intent that ministers needed were not part of who I was, or who I would ever be.

And secretly I was convinced I could never care enough. But even amid my refusal, I kept myself near the church. I joined task forces and the search committee and seminary boards because it kept me near the church. Near—but not too near. It was only in the months and years after Allen's birth that I could hear my call and answer it.

What was it about the birth of my children that broke my heart open, that entered in and made itself at home? It was this wondrous love. Love I had not counted on, love I could not have anticipated, love I had not earned, love I could not prove but knew was real. Daniel followed Allen and now there are these two people in my arms, climbing on my head, throwing themselves at me, clinging to my legs. There are these people who love me, even at 6:30 a.m., crabby and sleepy and distracted as I am. They do not keep score of all my failings. They see the me I long to be when I look in the mirror, and sometimes I think all my life since they were born has been the process of becoming that woman they see, the process of a woman, in Sonia Sanchez's words, "making pilgrimage to herself."

Mothering is about the business of worry and change and worrying about change. And though I may not be a world-class mother, I am a world-class worrier. The novelist Mary Gordon once wrote that being a mother means never again knowing a day without fear. I thought she was exaggerating, but she's been right so far. It also would be fair to say that her statement is not complete. The fear for them is real, and I expected that. But the fun of it, the joy, the incredible pride of knowing that these little people belong to you—and yet can never really belong to you—that, I did not expect. All these things—the fear and the joy—they shape and focus my life now. They imbue my life with a different kind of energy than I have known before. It is a palpable desire to make the world brand new for their sake. But it is difficult as I celebrate Mother's Day each year not to remember the millions of women who, along with me, would birth a new world if they could but have lost their faith in the very possibility of that world.

Lisbeth Schorr, a social analyst at Harvard University, has written two books; the most recent is entitled *Common Purpose*, and it was written as a kind of sequel to an earlier book, *Within Our Reach*.

Both these books have as their focus the intersection between social policy, good intentions, and the nature of bureaucracies. And though her analysis and her prescriptions have wide implications for a host of areas that concern us as citizens, Schorr's focus is relentlessly on children, especially poor and desperate children.

The premise of her previous book, *Within Our Reach*, is a simple one. She writes that after thirty years of social programs within the Great Society and beyond it, we know what works to change the lives of the disadvantaged people in our midst. She is vigorous in making the point that so many of us refuse to accept about social change. What we know how to do, what we could do tomorrow if only we would, are all the things that work not to *beat* the odds but to *change* the odds. It's long been Schorr's contention that we can't change everything in the lives of a poor child and her mother and father. But we can change enough things to give that family a fighting chance.

Schorr thus puts her finger on one of the most pernicious reasons we are failing the poor and the marginalized of this nation and this world, a reason we rarely utter even to ourselves. We are failing because we want to be perfect. Ever since the early 1980s when Ronald Reagan declared that "we fought a War on Poverty and poverty won," we have allowed ourselves to be sucked into the pernicious view that the poor will always be with us, so why bother. We've done all we can, and some of what's wrong with people in this country is that it's just part of their nature and will never change. This is an egregious lie, one fed by the personal conservative agendas of some, the discouragement of others, and the sheer exhaustion of still others who can barely figure out what to do with their own lives, much less someone else's.

The things we most need to change the world are some of the same things I've learned are needed as a mother and as a minister. For sure, they all take money, more money than you feel like you want to spend: sometimes they take more money than you really have. But mothering, ministry, changing the world—they take other things, too. They take practicality and flexibility, patience and humor, love and the right kind of accountability. They take a willingness to stand with one another, not in judgment but in profound and enduring faithfulness, as change takes place.

In her second book, *Common Purpose*, Schorr tells the story of a program called Homebuilders, a Tacoma, Washington, family intervention program that does remarkable work, in large part due to the concentrated time each staff person spends with the families entrusted to their care. At a weekly staff meeting, one of the workers made a request for $200 to help one of her families buy a washing machine. With an infant, two toddlers, and an incontinent aunt, the woman holding this family together didn't need therapy, an expensive home aide, or a bureaucratic song and dance as much as she needed a way not to haul clothes back and forth to the laundromat. So they helped to buy her a washing machine. In hearing this story later, a legal aid lawyer voiced the concern that the decision was irresponsible and unfair. Wasn't it a waste of money to help this family buy such an expensive item? And wouldn't every family then expect that same kind of help for some equally large purchase?

In fact, each member of the Homebuilders staff has discretionary power to effect just such purchases; that's one of the things that makes it a model program. Sometimes it means getting someone's car fixed so they can get to work. Sometimes it means getting a washing machine for a woman strained to the breaking point. Another Homebuilders worker recalls being met at the door by a new client who announced angrily that the last thing she needed in this world was another social worker showing up and telling her what to do. "What I really need to do is clean my house and get it in some kind of order," the woman said. So the social worker asked whether she would like them to start in the kitchen. And together the woman and the social worker cleaned her house and talked together about the troubles she was having with her teenaged daughter. Schorr makes it clear that, in all the programs that work, people are willing to do what's necessary to get the job done. What's necessary is not always heroic, or brave, or glamorous. But it does get the job done.

I would describe the process differently, I guess; I would say that Schorr gave us examples of hearts broken open and placed into the service of someone in need, not in that icky or condescending way that makes even the most earnest activist run for cover, but in the sensible, practical ways that mothers and fathers know, that ministers try to cultivate, that are the province of all of us who want the world to be different than it is.

When we are parenting, or ministering, to one another, how many have lost hope that things can really change? Our children often make us despair, the members of our families and communities don't see things our way and make us want to strangle them; the world we want to reconfigure resists and resists and resists. What, then, can be done? We can be faithful people. We can hang on. We can remember that standing with people, helping them to bear their burdens, accompanying them, is one of the tools that makes a changed life possible.

I'm lucky to have a faithful mother who stood with me on days when she could hardly stand for herself. I remember that about her all the time, not just on Mother's Day each year as I wear a red carnation in her honor. Because I know all too well that not everyone has a mother like that, it's what I'll treasure about her all my life. Because of her example, I work hard to be a faithful mother, and I hope it's what my children eventually think of when they think of me. I hope, too, that they learn to see my faithfulness not only in my life with them, but also in my life in the world outside our home, where the need for faithfulness takes a different shape but is just as great. And on each Mother's Day, in what I hope is a very long time from now, I like to think they'll pin white carnations to their lapels and remember that they were the reasons I wanted to change the world. I pray they'll wear their white carnations and think of me—and pick up where I left off.

Betsy Wharton

The Rabbi's Garage

I had seen Rabbi Wolfe-Blank only twice, and always from a distance. The first time, my husband, Rob, son, Forrest, and I stood among a crowd of thirty along the bank of an urban lake in Seattle. It was *Tashlikh*, the afternoon service during *Rosh ha-Shanah* when Jews traditionally gather to cast away regrets, like bread tossed into murky water to be eaten by fish and transformed. Undistracted by the intermittent whizz of lycra-clad skaters and the cheerful parade of parents with strollers, Rabbi David blew the *Shofar* and led us through an eclectic service of prayer, melodic chanting and dance. The service concluded as we tossed our handful of bread into the lake, then sat in the warm September grass to contemplate regrets and transformation.

A year later we attended another service: *Kol Nidre*, the night that begins the *Yom Kippur* day of fasting. Rabbi Wolfe-Blank, dressed in white robes, his head and shoulders draped with a brightly colored prayer shawl, recited the somber prayers of atonement. The congregation swayed and rocked as they *davened* the Hebrew melody. I felt myself absorbed, taken up by the chanting around us.

Intrigued by this rabbi and this congregation, we considered affiliating. But in the nine years since our mixed-faith marriage we had not yet resolved the question of religion. Christianity or Judaism? Or even the neutrality of Buddhism where neither one of us

211

had history. One of these days. Before we have a child. Before we have a second child. But our stubborn aversion to organized faith and the immediately compelling demands of work, childcare and good ski seasons had always usurped our attention. Until that is, the birth of our second son.

I am lying in a hospital bed, on my right side, gripping the hard steel railing. The distant pulse of a new contraction gathers strength, and I go inward to meet the pain. There is a yellow dahlia in a vase brought from home, the last of the season. I fix my gaze on the petals. I breathe in and count one petal. Inhale deeply, exhale slowly. Around and around in a spiral moving outward. Each petal a breath. I reach the outer edge of the bloom as the pain recedes. Now rest. Rob wipes the sweat from my face with a cool washrag. He rubs my back. He is proud of me; and I am strengthened by him. And then I feel the next wave, so soon and more intense than the last. I gasp in pain and I snarl, "Don't touch me."

Inhale petals, start in the center, spiral outward, exhale slowly.

I want to push now. But the nurse tells me to wait. I can't control this any longer. I can't slow it down. It's time. The baby's coming. Oh my god! My body heaves, forcing out a moan, a low and loud and deep utterance. There is only pain. I am splitting apart.

"It's a boy," a voice cries out. And then softly, "he has a little cleft," as if this were a small detail like the color of his hair or a sweet freckle. To my left a nurse lays the baby on the warming table. A mask conceals her face. I see competent hands, a stethoscope. "Call anesthesiology," she shouts, "I'm not getting a pulse." She begins CPR, tapping out quick beats with two fingers on the baby's chest.

"Let's get him to the nursery." Rob follows the baby as they roll him out the door.

Now I am alone—naked, bleeding, shivering, cold, and alone. The predictable waves of pain have stopped. My labor is complete, but there is no relief. I came here expecting joy. Everything is silent. I've lost my place.

I wore wool socks as we walked down the hall toward the neonatal intensive care unit. Grim faces peered at us from the periphery. Rob told me what he knew. The cleft palate could be repaired. But there were other anomalies: twelve fingers and toes, a heart defect, abnormal eyes and kidneys. He was breathing too fast, and they didn't know why. Tomorrow an ambulance would take him to Children's Hospital.

We stood beside the incubator, tears rolling down our cheeks. Our new son, the one we had called Pearl all these months — small treasure growing inside, the one we had hoped for, planned for, dreamed of, our perfect possibility was disfigured.

We had planned to call him Samuel after his great-grandfather, but considering our child's unlucky future, we hesitated. And then we named him: Samuel.

Exhausted but unable to sleep, I sat in a rocking chair, touching the steel frame of his crib with my hand. Separated by glass and fear and grief, I wanted to howl, like some she wolf that had been robbed of her cub. I ached to take my baby into my arms, to draw him back inside my body where he had been all mine, all perfection. I wanted to smell him. I wanted to bury my face in the soft folds of his skin and lick him clean.

A nurse offered a glass of cool water and then, finally, allowed me to hold the baby. "He's stable now. It'll do you both some good."

In my arms, swaddled in flannel, my son's newborn head rested on the sleeve of my blue and white hospital robe. I leaned to stroke his face with my cheek. Unspeakable softness. I inhaled the sweet air of his breath.

"Samuel," I whispered. My tongue rolled around the unfamiliar name. "Samuel. Sam. Sammy. Sammy, you're not what I expected."

I counted his toes: six toes. I counted them again. I stroked the length of his legs and wrapped a hand around the width of his new thigh. Sammy opened his eyes, and I peered into the keyhole shape of his irises, "Can you see me, Sammy?" With my index finger I touched the frightening outline of his gaping upper lip — his mouth and nostrils merged into one. Inhale fear. Exhale calm.

On the slope of his forehead I noticed a swirl of hair, like the Milky Way. Another deep breath and the weight in my chest lightened. I gently traced the coppery fine swirl of hair around and around. And then for a moment, my fear was suspended.

Kneeling beside the manger,
Mother Mary sees the excruciating future
Written in her son's face.
She reaches out and takes him into her arms.
As if caressed by an angel, she is reassured by the softness
    of skin.
Shepherds arrive and see a halo shining

In the morning, Forrest, age five, came to meet his baby brother for the first time. Rob and I prepared answers, nervously practicing simple phrases and half truths, "Your brother is a little different than we expected. He needs to stay at the hospital for a while. Is there anything you want to ask?"

"Can I touch him?" Forrest leaned over the armrest of the rocking chair where I sat holding the baby. His feet dangled off the ground.

"Of course you can, honey. Just be gentle." Forrest kissed his new brother on the forehead and took hold of one of his hands. He studied him for a while then said, "Hey mommy! Six plus six is twelve. And twelve is my favorite number!"

"Polydactyly, or the presence of extra fingers and toes, is common in patients with Trisomy 13," explained Dr. Sterling Clarren, Chief of Dismorphology at the University of Washington Medical Center. Results of the genetic studies had come in that morning. Rob and I sat close together on a couch in the shadowy conference room. Sammy was five days old.

Trisomy 13 is a severe genetic defect in which every cell in the body carries an extra chromosome. Every cell and therefore every organ system carries the flaw. "Most often," Dr. Sterling continued, "Trisomy 13 pregnancies result in miscarriage." With this he turned to me with a look of admiration and said, "You must have had a healthy pregnancy; Samuel is the most robust Trisomy 13 we've ever seen here. He surprised us."

Indeed.

Ninety percent of infants born with Trisomy 13 succumb within the first year. Occasionally, and with intensive medical intervention, some live longer. The doctor told us with careful optimism that he'd read of a patient that had survived eleven years. Later, I read the article myself and learned that the patient, a little girl, had been hospitalized more than one hundred times. I could imagine her mother keeping count of each one of those hospital stays.

He told us that victims of Trisomy 13 rarely experience pain. Nor do they talk, laugh or walk. He showed us a picture of a child dragging himself along on an exercise bar in a rehab center. But, he added, the child in the photo had a less severe form. Of course, anything is possible. Research is ongoing. It was also possible, said the doctor that Sammy would not be able to swallow and possible that his respiratory problems could worsen, in which case a ventilator could sustain him.

He did not show us any more photographs.

The walls at Children's Hospital are painted with
    bright-colored murals
depicting jungle animals riding on a train:
elephants, toucans, and smiling tigers.

We brought Sammy home. As we parked the car in front of our house, neighbors appeared and helped us unload. Sammy came home with an oxygen tank and a pulse oximeter, a machine to monitor the oxygen in his blood. There was also a feeding pump and an I.V. pole and a custom-built foam wedge on which he was supposed to sleep. Each machine came with the requisite box of supplies: tape and tubing, bottles of normal saline, and syringes. Together we converted his freshly painted room into a hospital ward.

On some days it was the tubing I hated the most. There were two kinds, one carried oxygen and the other breast milk; both were taped to his left cheek. The nurse at the hospital had called the feeding machine a "handy little backpack unit." True, it was encased in sturdy blue pack cloth and it did have a shoulder strap. I tried to imagine a simple hike with gorp, sunscreen, Swiss army knife, feeding machine and portable oxygen tank.

Six times a day every day I pumped breast milk. Normally, they teach you to visualize your baby's face to stimulate the pituitary gland to release the hormone Prolactin that causes the letdown of milk. The first night, standing at the kitchen counter, my bare feet cold on the linoleum floor, I closed my eyes and visualized my Sammy's face, his nose and mouth merged into one gaping opening, plastic tubes and tape. Instead of milk, I felt the warm splash of teardrops hitting my feet. Eventually, I learned my own method. I prayed as I pumped. In truth I didn't really know how to pray, but I learned to listen. In between the inhale and the exhale, as the electric pump rhythmically squeezed and whirred, I noticed the silence. I searched the stillness for direction. For ten minutes every four hours I sat quietly. I breathed deeply, and I produced a lot of milk. After a few weeks, dozens of eight-ounce storage bags filled our freezer. I produced so much milk that I had to store some of it across the street at my neighbor's house.

During those days I wrote in a journal every chance I could get. Usually, I started with some particular heaviness or a poignant moment. I took it to the page, and very often in the writing I would find some kind of peace. But as the bouquets of flowers faded and the days and sleepless nights of caregiving wore on, it became more and more difficult for me to find the generosity, the lightness of spirit I needed in order to accept my son's disabilities. Medical appointments, pumping milk and Sammy's crying defined my days. He cried almost constantly, despite our attentions. I began to feel a sense of imprisonment. Sammy's needs dictated my life, our family's life. Eventually, even the writing couldn't lift me up. I have read back over the entries in the notebook from those days and I am shocked by my words.

> October 30: If I were a gerbil, I would eat this defective offspring and at least recoup the nutrients …
>
> November 10: I had a dream last night. I was a child dressed in a Girl Scout uniform and I had drawn a picture with a crayon. I folded it in half again and again and finally I took it to the wastebasket, tore it into pieces and said, "It just didn't come out the way I wanted."
>
> November 15: I am afraid he might die. I am terrified he might live.
>
> December 2: We simply do what we can to survive. Just the basics, rock the baby; stay with the breath. Hold one another. Seek guidance.

Seeking guidance, I called the rabbi:

"Shalom and thank you for calling Congregation Eitz Or. If you'd like to leave a message for Rabbi David Wolfe-Blank, you may do so after the tone."

"Hello, my name is Betsy Wharton. I have a question … about God. You don't know me, but our new baby is sick. Well, he might die, but he might live and … Could we talk to you?"

He came to our house that night. He wore a nylon jacket, khaki pants and canvas shoes, his graying hair barely covered by a crocheted *yamulke*. In the intimate space of our living room we made awkward introductions. Rabbi David asked to hold the baby and despite the complexity of Sammy's tubes, he settled comfortably on the couch and gazed serenely at the baby as we spoke. Rob and Forrest snuggled together in a chair. I brought a stool in from the kitchen, and we tried to explain.

Rabbi David said he didn't know anything much about deformity or illness, said that personally he really couldn't handle death, avoided it mostly. He told us that he'd missed the funeral of a beloved friend. He regretted it now, but he just couldn't make himself go.

Sammy rattled and gurgled, and began to cry. Rabbi David handed the baby to me as he continued to speak. I stood swaying back and forth, listening. Casually, Rabbi David began to tell a story. I believe he said it was a *midrash* from the Bal Shem Tov.

A very good man died. In his long life he had completed 612 of the required 613 mitzvot or commandments required for admittance to heaven. So, with only one more mitzvah to complete, his soul returned to earth, took another birth. Rabbi David explained that to the mystics, the soul is the fragment of light that enlivens us. Sammy's — mine — Rabbi David's. No less, no more. This time, because he only had that one last mitzvah to complete, the man did not need very much time in his new life. And he didn't need the full range of human abilities. He only needed enough to complete that one last mitzvah.

The conversation moved on. Sammy had fallen asleep. I felt the perfect warmth of his body as he wriggled in closer to my breast. I studied his face. Cleft palate: a midline defect. It was time to irrigate, to remove the accumulation of mucous that impeded his breath, and moisten the inflamed membranes of his nasal septum, tissue that was ill-equipped for this constant exposure to the drying air. A friend had recently remarked that she thought his mouth was beautiful, like a vase inviting her to place a small rosebud in the opening. I considered the possibility that Sammy had everything that he needed. No more, and no less. Just enough for one mitzvah.

And I began to believe that what I had to give would also be enough.

My friend Colleen came over to visit one afternoon. I was holding Sammy in my arms as I opened the front door. Just as she walked in, Sammy stopped breathing. He had begun to have periods of apnea — the cessation of breath. Sometimes it would last for a minute, sometimes several minutes. Colleen and I watched together as his face grew pale, then dusky purple. He was so still, unbelievably still. Instinctively I held my breathe with him, but I couldn't last that long. We waited. Neither of us moved. After a while Sammy came back. He stretched and opened his eyes and began to cry. I looked up at Colleen's stricken face. Together we wept. My child was dying.

> Noah and his family huddled together in the ark for forty days
>   and forty nights
> while the rain came down.
> Moses and his people wandered in the desert for forty years
> in search of the promised land.
> Jesus prayed in the desert for forty days
> before returning to Jerusalem.
> And Sammy lived for forty days before he died.

Rabbi David came by that evening to talk, and drink whiskey and weep and laugh and muse about the birth and death of our sweet baby. The date was December 8, and it was also Reb David's birthday, but he had come just the same; he told us what to do. He told us to stay home. He said to watch our dreams, because the windows between the worlds had been opened twice for Sammy: once for him to cross in and once again for him to cross out.

At the funeral we ripped our clothes and said *Kaddish*. Afterward we washed our hands, ate a hard-boiled egg and lit the seven-day memorial candle. We covered the mirrors and we stayed home. It was a rare time. Rob and I lay on our bed and read poetry to each other. When the candle burned out, we uncovered the mirrors and found our faces swollen and pale. We took the traditional first walk around the neighborhood, enjoying the cold wet December air and the kind attentions of our neighbors. Upon returning, the house felt empty. I cleaned Sammy's room. We took down the crib. Now what?

Wednesday Nights at 7 p.m.: a series of classes with Rabbi David Wolfe-Blank on Jewish Prayer. Classes to be held in Reb David's garage.

Rob and I walked across wet grass in the winter darkness to a small garage behind the house. Unsure, we checked the address on the flyer, then knocked on the only door. We were met by a blast of over-heated air, the squinting glare of a single light bulb overhead and the curious looks of more than a dozen students squeezed around a rectangular table. Rabbi David, perched on a bar stool, smiled directly at me as if we had just shared a joke.

"We can fit four on this couch," a man said kindly as he adjusted his glasses and wriggled his large frame closer to the woman beside him. Despite my desire to stay close to Rob, I smiled and sidestepped along the wall towards the couch. I sank deeply into the worn velour between two men. They introduced themselves. Both were named Irving. Rob took a folding chair and wedged himself into a corner.

I can't remember what Reb David spoke about that first night. The suffocating air and my own bewilderment at being out in the world, and page after page of double-sided Xerox distracted me from the discussions.

It had been seven weeks since Sammy's birth. I could still feel the sting of my torn labia, and the oozing release of clotted blood. It had been ten days since his death. I sat with my shoulders squeezed between the two Irvings; my breasts ached with the weight of unnecessary milk. I felt vulnerable and raw, my skin too thin. I wanted to bolt out of there and breathe deeply of the cold night air. I couldn't last an hour without crying. But I stayed.

Weeks went by. Rob and I continued to attend the class, not every week but often enough. We studied the Hebrew and English translations of various prayers. Interpretations of interpretations: Reconstructionist, Reform, Conservative, Kabbalistic, Renewal, and Orthodox. Rabbi David consulted thick texts, fondly naming their authors with real familiarity: commentary upon commentary. He casually mentioned the strict order in which books should be stacked, then diverged off into the multiple meanings of words written without vowels. I realized that I was in the presence of a scholar.

One night Rabbi David led us through a *Siddur* Drama, or reenactment, of the evening prayer.

Barukh atah Adonai, ha-ma-ariv aravim
Blessed are you, Creator of the Universe, the One
Rolling away light, bringing on the darkness.

All these years of my Jewish half-life, words such as these had always held little meaning to me. And now, there I was standing in a theater of prayer, myself an actor invited to play the audacious part of the divine creator. Half of the class played the face of darkness; the rest took the part of the light. The two groups stood opposite, and with graceful arms we caused the sun to set and the moon to rise. Like a giving and receiving, we made the stars come out. We pierced through the darkness. Then like a wave receding, we rolled away the darkness and made way for light. We did this, not just once, but over and over again, day after night after day, until the rhythm of the world permeated us. Creator and Created. Why and how? It didn't matter. Only the rhythm.

We got the phone call on a Friday night. A car accident: Reb David's Suburu went off the road, coming home from vacation on Vancouver Island. Rolled three times. Head injury. Brain dead. They would withdraw life support tomorrow evening after the Sabbath, at sunset. Elaine, his wife, had a cracked vertebra. Their son, Uri, age five, uninjured except that he would have to start kindergarten the next week without his father.

Driving through the hilly wheat country of the Palouse in Eastern Washington, I don't remember where I was headed. Sunset patches of golden wheat alternated with black unplanted soil as the earth slowly rotated towards night. Just another evening, and God was rolling away the light to make way for darkness, to make way for light again. Squinting into the blazing horizon, I strained to see the road ahead. I thought about Rabbi David, and I wondered if it was sunset when his car went off the road. I thought about Sammy; it had been almost a year since his birth. I rolled down my window to enjoy the feel of hot rushing wind. I wondered if Reb David had his car window open. Brilliant orange gave way to searing red, then gorgeous purple.

With a single stroke, the sleeve of God transforms the world from day to night—every day, over and again. It has been this way since the beginning, and it will continue until the end. Darkness rolls away light. It occurred to me that rolling is too mild a word. It sometimes feels more like peeling, or ripping, or skinning me alive. Red of my torn flesh, and purple of my bruised spirit.

Driving into the coming night, my eyes filled with tears. Unable to see, I pulled off to the side of the road. I cried alone in the cab of my pickup. In darkness except for the occasional approach of headlights, I waited for my vision to clear.

A year has passed and now it is spring. My new baby girl Maya plays in the grassy sunshine. She walks on unsteady legs, and with her arms outstretched, she grips a half-eaten strawberry in one hand. The wheelbarrow catches her attention. It is filled with garden soil, hand trowel, my favorite spade, some clay pots. She plunges her greedy hands into the wet dirt. I think about stopping her; but she is delighted with her exploration. Now Maya straightens up, still grasping the blackened strawberry, holding it up high, waving it about like a prize. She smiles so wide it seems her face will split apart.

Then she jams the strawberry into her mouth. Bits of mud and sticky red juice run down her chin. She looks at me bewildered, her smile breaks. Her anticipation is betrayed, and she begins to cry. I scoop her up in my arms and hold her close, clearing the bits of dirt out of her mouth. "You're okay, sweet lamb." I say, holding back laughter, "Take a deep breath. You're all right."

Sarah Conover

Orthopraxy

G od dammit you kids, we're late for church again!" Clutch-ing the Vista Cruiser's arm rests, seat-beltless, peering past Dad's looming figure in the front seat, I prayed. Snow banked the sidewalks; ice glazed the roads. My sisters and I jammed willy-nilly against each other, thrown side-to-side in the back seat. Rac-ing to Larchmont Presbyterian Church on Sundays stands out as my childhood's most sincere moments of prayer.

Yet the instant we stepped inside, all changed. When the heavy church doors shut behind us, the family strife remained outside, left in the frigid air. An ancient fragrance of mahogany and teak enveloped us; the rose window—a jeweled kaleidoscope thirty feet in diameter—beckoned me forward. A lacework of carved arches, both stone and wood, seemed to cradle the pews with pre-ordained symmetry. The subdued glow of gothic lanterns dangled far above from the ceiling's mysterious, dark firmament.

The contrast boggled my mind, and as I grew older, the par-adoxes demanded answers: How and where do the two worlds merge? Can religions successfully weave together the secular and the sacred? Is it possible? Can the solace found in a church, where *kairos*—sacred time—reigns, be carried palpably into the chaotic hours of each day, into *chronos*? And thus began the pur-suit of my life's central question.

In time, I became the parent behind the steering wheel—only

infrequently headed to church—but chronically frantic, late, and often as angry as Dad. Parenting, I now know, has a stubborn way of ushering to the forefront aspects of our psyches most in need of attention. Just like I saw in my father, the reconciliation of a breathless American pace with my idea of a spiritually centered life seemed unimaginable.

My first child, Nate, brought big ontological issues to the dinner table just about as soon as he had words. "How can we be sure this life is not a dream?" he asked at three. "How do you know we're not dreaming now, and that your dreams at night aren't the real world?" Indeed. My second child, Jamey, entering the world as vivacious as she is stubborn, made a spiritual practice inescapable. Finding a way to stumble through parenthood without my ideals chasmed from daily life became my sole focus.

When I was pregnant with our first child, my husband Doug and I moved from Colorado, our home for many years, to California. There may be no better place on earth than California to sample the world's bouquet of religions: highly cultivated heirloom blooms bunched side-by-side with wind-pollinated, unpredictable hybrids. Despite a degree in comparative religions and a major in Eastern wisdom traditions, I felt a strong tug to honor and pass on our Judeo-Christian roots. With each season came an irresistible childhood holiday memory—spring's chartreuse intermingled with a riot of dyed Easter eggs, winter's darkness lifted by pungent swags of evergreens—and a decision to establish, or not, similar rituals with our new family.

Nate's easy nature from infancy onward made our exploration of religions leisurely. We sampled a spectrum of churches—from the renowned Glide Memorial to the Friends' Society to the Unitarian Universalists. We liked them all. Under the soulful spell of gospel music, I jumped right into Glide's social justice programs; the Friends' Society and the Unitarians drew colorful, intellectual congregations also involved in the community. What was not to like?

But with Jamey's birth, our family plunged into a divide just like that of my childhood—between two extremes. Nate, who complied with every request, who could concentrate on a picture book alone for an hour or build a Lego car by himself, gave Doug and me the mistaken idea that we could write the definitive parenting manual. Jamey's first word, on the other hand, as she reached her palms toward us like two greedy animals, was "more!" A force of nature was let loose in our lives. It was as if we spoke opposite languages from our daughter: no meant yes; don't meant do; come here definitely meant flee. We found ourselves behaving much like the fathers from whose dictatorial reigns we'd both run. The dawning realization of that fact devastated us. It brought Doug and me to a desperate search for an every day, every hour, every minute spiritual practice. Our days of religio-tourism were over.

The beginning of the help we sought turned up just a few miles down the road from our Fairfax, California, home at Spirit Rock Center. In a pastoral setting of oaks and rolling coastal foothills, Spirit Rock is one of the primary hubs of American Buddhism. I listened to the simple meditation instructions. I uncrossed my legs, felt the shape of the chair like a supporting hand, and closed my eyes. A quilt of silence enveloped the packed room. I marveled at my breath, a silky streamlet flowing in and out. After some time, my frantic thoughts dropped away. The gentle downward pressure of gravity, of each foot planted beneath me, felt like the foundation I had been looking for. When I returned home, I told Doug, "I think I found what we've been looking for."

Through attention to our ordinary moment-by-moment experience, Buddhism soon became a lifeboat for us to gain some perspective and equanimity. Doug and I learned to meditate and became familiar with various aspects of Buddhist philosophy and practice. For the kids, teaching them a little about Buddhism sufficed for now; but for Doug and me, an orthopraxy of meditation—an everyday corrective action as opposed to faith in a dogma—became an imperative.

Then, in 1992, we moved to rural, conservative, northeast Washington State. We planted an orchard and acres of alfalfa, fashioned raised-beds of flowers and vegetables, bought a flock of chicks, strung a zip line in the barn from a tower of hay bales to the trampoline, and purchased a pregnant mare. We anticipated a pastoral, idyllic situation.

Yet at some point during the second grade, Nate returned from his new school with elaborate, apocalyptic tales of sword fights between Jesus and Satan. Once, I felt forced to call a parent and request that her son stop telling Jamey she was going to burn in hell. "Well, he is just concerned about her!" said the mom. Ironically, the situation became the ultimate ready-made lesson on tolerance and gave us opportunities to discuss world religions, prejudice, fanaticism, and war.

Isolated from our previous *sangha*, our Buddhist community, Doug and I created family rituals and improvised new traditions. We began a silent Sunday evening meal with a blessing written by Thich Nhat Hanh, a Buddhist monk nominated for the Nobel Peace Prize. It took heroic impulse control for our spirited child to tap the brass bell softly, or to stop mouthing, "Can we talk yet? Can we talk now? How about now?" A struggle to be sure, but nothing like the usual dinners, where she would not sit down for more than half a minute and a heated blowout would ensue. The once-a-week custom seemed to change the frame enough for her to respect the quiet, briefly, and even sit through the whole meal.

Looking for a comforting bedtime ritual, we began a nighttime *metta*, or loving-kindness prayer. The solace of candlelight set the stage. We sat in silence together for a minute or so, spoke a wish for our own happiness, and then widened the circle to include all beings, especially anyone we've been angry with. Nate often waxed philosophical. Here's one of his prayers I uncovered in an old journal of mine: "May we all peel away layers of judgment that we have around someone so that we can notice the special things about him or her." Another journal entry shows Jamey's sparkle. It describes how, as I spoke my wishes for myself, then outward to our community, our beautiful state—its land, plants, and animals—all nations, the oceans, and finally, all beings everywhere, Jamey blurted out an exuberant, "You go girl!"

None of our homemade rituals have been perfect for Jamey's disposition—a minute of meditation feels like an eternity to her. She complains that Buddhism is too peaceful, too boring. She groans when we announce silent dinner. Nevertheless, we managed to extend the lengths of silence. And for me, within that quiet rested the kernel of a long-sought goal: the opportunity to blend *kairos*, sacred time, with an ordinary activity.

In truth, these traditions were respites from the more common tenor of family life. Blending *kairos* with *chronos* might just be another way of speaking about the quality of life—especially the quality of family life in the hardest moments—when the path you hoped you'd walk with your children diverges into the runoff ditch full of generational rubbish. Doug and I spent a lot of time in that ditch, cleaning ourselves off and then climbing back out. We lay awake many nights vowing to be better parents: in the future we'd pause for twenty seconds before responding to Jamey's obstinacy; next time we'd simply walk away from a conflict and not engage in argument; from now on we'd preempt a full-on tantrum with an automatic consequence for even raising her voice. The strategies worked with various degrees of success. Temporarily.

There's a Tibetan Buddhist story of a famous *rinpoche*, or teacher, who roamed the Himalayas about a century ago, disguised in beggar's rags. He entered the cave of a monk who had sequestered himself for twenty years in hopes of perfecting patience. The roaming monk began to pester him: he complained that meditation is boring; he wanted something to drink; he asked him about the view from the cave; he was hungry; he wanted to know what the cave monk thought about all day long. He chattered incessantly until the cave monk exploded, demanding to be left in peace. The rinpoche retorted, "I'd be glad to leave, but it looks like your patience left first."

Jamey, we decided, was our roaming monk, badgering us until she got a noticeable response, continually testing the depth of our inner work.

Doug and I inherited years of conditioning that children needed to comply with adult demands. Now that I have distance and both kids have fledged, I can look back and admire Jamey's contrariness. A memory comes to me of when she stood up to the family matriarch. Once again, she was heckling her brother relentlessly—one of her very favorite pastimes—in the presence of both sets of grandparents.

Matriarch: "You are a nasty little girl!"

Jamey: "Well, you're just a cranky old lady and I don't like you anyway!" She was no older than four. I didn't admonish her for impoliteness that time; I admired her stunning truthfulness when it wasn't aimed at me.

How do we change our conditioned responses from the wounds inflicted by our families of origin so that we don't harm our own children? Either parenting becomes our spiritual practice, or we bequeath the damage to another generation. In some ways, becoming "Buddhists," with the cultural freight of idealized Asian composure, may have made our internal struggle all the worse because we kept falling so far short. But we did our best to have an everyday spiritual practice, and I know both children saw this; when things went awry, when the yelling ended and the discipline was doled out, Doug and I each had to face a penance that inevitably presented itself during meditation. An apology from us was usually the result.

Doug says he knows the exact moment when parenting and Buddhism switched places as the focus of his inner work. I was at a meditation retreat, and he at home with the kids. Jamey, a tween, had earned herself a large consequence for one thing or another. Doug said she was grounded for the weekend. Her response was to walk out the door without a glance behind. The amount of rage Doug felt at that moment contrasted so sharply with my working my "spirituality" in a cabin in the woods, alone, that it brought the real priority into focus: parenting as the spiritual path.

For me, the transformation happened as I cringed before the looming horizon of a damaged relationship with my daughter in her last years before leaving us. During her junior year of high school, Doug and I had scheduled a counseling appointment to figure out the consequences for the biggest crisis she had brought yet to the family. List-like, we went over every punishment we'd ever used. The therapist added to our list. We'd already tried those too, but had just forgotten. Nothing had prevented the present catastrophe.

Then, it was if the room's miasma brightened with an essential insight: We'd tried every natural consequence, every behavioral strategy we could think of for years; all we had left was relationship-building with our daughter. Love, not control.

Seeing Jamey's indomitable spirit as a "problem" needing a "solution" was mistaken. Alan Watts, that sideways teacher of Buddhism, pointed out that problems are to be solved, but mysteries are to be enjoyed unsolved—that we would be much better off, and happier, if we regarded the universe and existence itself as mysteries. Countless times I looked at both my children—at every age of their growing—stunned by the miracle of their being, kairos fully present as I remained present, watching. How easy it is to forget that mystery in the midst of messy chronos, in the midst of trying the best we know how to keep our children out of trouble.

It seemed as soon as Doug and I changed, so did our daughter. The fall semester of her senior year Jamey brought home a perfect report card. She sought out our company, even for public outings at the mall, as if she, too, knew our last months together were precious. She apologized for misunderstandings before I did. A short six months later, her first letters back from college declared that we were "the best parents, the best people ever," and she wondered, "How had we put up with her?"

I've been a seeker since adolescence, exploring a variety of wisdom traditions, looking for reconciliation between the real and ideal. It felt odd building new rituals from Eastern religions, from sources foreign to my own youth. But parenting upped the stakes so that I had to find some way to diminish my own suffering and the contingent suffering of those around me. Our culture is a shared, woven cloth we wrap ourselves in. To cut holes in that fabric feels like wielding scissors a little recklessly, gambling that there will be new patches to fit. In time, some of my childhood's Christian magic, its celebrations and teachings, seeped organically to the surface, becoming part of our family life—a twinkling Christmas tree in one corner of the living room, a Buddha on the mantle with woolen hat, scarf, and mittens. For the interconnected times in which we live, there may be no reasonable choice other than to appreciate, study, and learn from the world's diverse, holy geography—the ways, I believe, everyone is trying to reconcile kairos and chronos. Our most sacred duty is to attempt it as an orthopraxy for our families.

Hopey Stories

Paradox
I am a hopeful man this morning because a dear friend died the other day. His name was Bob. His heart finally shut down after eighty-five years. He died the last day of summer. He'd been working in his garden, editing garlic. His death rattles and harrows me, his absence pains me exceedingly, and the loss of his savory company is a hole unfillable; yet, as the days pass, and his death becomes more story and less wound, I grow more hopeful. It doesn't make sense: How does a great loss produce hope? But his character has bones in it, his patience was a sea, his pursuit of clarity relentless, his humor gentle and thorough. I look at it this way: As a species, we produced a Bob, we Bobbed, we were Bobbified. A very good sign for *homo sapiens* as a verb through time, a project in process, that one of its little-known individual members was extraordinary stuff. Makes you realize there are a lot of little-known extraordinary individuals. Says a lot for possibility.

Expedition
On the lip of the misnamed Pacific, on a bright afternoon, a man and his three small sandy children are shuffling south along the strand. They are following a line of seawrack left by the tide. Wrack ingredients: shatters of shells, crab-legs, fish-bones, the debreasted bodies of gulls and young murres, and seaweed of all shapes and

sizes, from bright-green filmy sea-spinach to the enormously long kelp whips all three children are dragging like the rubbery brown tails of herculean mice. Every footfall along the wrack-line raises a leaping herd of what we call beach fleas or sand hoppers—tiny translucent animals with major-league spring. One of my small twin sons and I plop down for a visit with the hoppers. We catch a few, stare into their eyes, conduct Hopper Olympics. Later, as I am bookishly chasing scholarly names for the hoppers (maritime semiterrestrial talitrid gammarid amphipod crustacea, *megalorchestia*), I hear this son explaining to a listener that he and his dad had a lot of fun on the beach: "We found some beach hopers," says the boy. "Hoppers?" asks audience. "No, hopers," says boy; "they hope right up in the air when they see giants. They're hopey."

Peeroration
On the same beach on another day the same four people are digging in the sand. The two youngest, boys, twins, are digging pee-holes, which they post-pee fill neatly, as conscientiously pee-prim as dogs. The daughter, older, conscious of dignity, disdainful of her brothers' headlongitude, is digging for mole crabs (*Emerita analoga*), who burrow backward into the sand in the swash zone, unfurl feathery antennae, and net infinitesimal food. In an hour father and daughter dig up more than a hundred crabs, in less than a square yard of beach. The father, agog at the squirming populace, begins to calculate how many small mole crabs there might be in the whole cove. Pretty soon his head hurts, but he finds himself cheerful: That's a lot of lives.

Why hope, how hope, in a culture inured to death, a world fouling its nest, a politics driven by greed? Because there are giants; because there are children; because life leaps.

About the Contributors

MARTHA BECK is the author of several international bestsellers, including *Expecting Adam* and *Finding Your Own North Star*, as well as *Steering By Starlight*. She is also a monthly columnist for *O, The Oprah Magazine*. She has taught a variety of subjects at Harvard and the American Graduate School of International Management. She lives with her family in Phoenix, Arizona.

D.S. BUTTERWORTH lives in Spokane, Washington, where he teaches writing and literature at Gonzaga University. His work has appeared in many literary journals. His books include the nonfiction work *Waiting for Rain: A Farmer's Story* and a book of poetry, *The Radium Watch Dial Painters*, published in 2008.

NADINE CHAPMAN teaches creative writing and composition at Whitworth College in Spokane, Washington. Her recent work includes a poetry chapbook, *On Solitude* (Finishing Line Press, Summer 2005). Her short stories about women in north central Idaho have appeared in journals such as *Weber Studies* and *Frontiers: A Journal of Women Studies*. She spent her childhood in Anchorage, Alaska, and on the Aleutian Islands, where her father operated a cattle ranch. Before teaching writing, she worked as a psychiatric registered nurse in Anchorage and Berkeley, California. During the summer, she travels with her husband and children to their farm on the Camas Prairie in Idaho.

SARAH CONOVER holds a BA in Religious Studies from the University of Colorado and an MFA in Creative Writing from Eastern Washington University. Her poems and essays have been published in various literary magazines and anthologies. She is the author and/or co-author of four books on world religions— *Kindness: A Treasury of Buddhist Wisdom for Children and Parents*; *Daughters of the Desert: Stories of Remarkable Women from the Christian, Jewish and Muslim Traditions*; *Ayat Jamilah: Beautiful Signs, a Treasury of Islamic Wisdom for Children and Parents*; and *Harmony: A Treasury of Chinese Wisdom for Children and Parents*. Sarah lives in Spokane, Washington, with her husband, Doug Robnett. Both their children have fledged the nest and are attending college. Sarah teaches creative writing to teens and elders—now and then, both at the very same time.

BRIAN DOYLE edits *Portland Magazine* at the University of Portland in Oregon—the best university magazine in America, according to *Newsweek*. Doyle is the author of ten books: five collections of essays, two nonfiction books, two collections of "proems," and the sprawling novel *Mink River*. His greatest accomplishments are that a riveting woman said *yup* when he mumbled a marriage proposal, that the Coherent Mercy then sent them three lanky, snotty, sneery, testy, sweet, brilliant, nutty, muttering children in skin boats from the sea of the stars.

GERALD EARLY is a noted essayist and American culture critic. His collections of essays include *Tuxedo Junction: Essays on American Couture*; *The Culture of Bruising: Essays on Prizefighting, Literature and Modern American Culture*, which won the 1994 National Book Critics Circle Award for Criticism; and *This Is Where I Came In: Essays on Black America in the 1960s*. His essays have also been widely anthologized. He is the Merle Kling Professor of Modern Letters in the Department of English and director of the Center of the Humanities at Washington University in St. Louis, where he has taught since 1982.

ALEXANDRA FULLER is the author of *Don't Let's Go to the Dogs Tonight: An African Childhood*, a *New York Times* Notable Book of 2002, and a finalist for the *Guardian* First Book Award; *Scribbling the Cat*; and the *Legend of Colton H. Bryant*. Her articles and reviews have appeared in numerous publications. Fuller lives in Wyoming with her husband and three children.

DEBRA GWARTNEY is the author of the memoir *Live Through This*. She is a member of the nonfiction writing faculty at Portland State University in Oregon, and is co-editor, with Barry Lopez, of *Home Ground: Language for an American Landscape*, published in 2006 by Trinity University Press. Her short stories, personal narratives, essays, and articles have appeared in numerous magazines and journals. Debra lives in Western Oregon with her husband, the writer Barry Lopez. She is the mother of four grown daughters.

JONATHAN JOHNSON is the author of *Hannah and the Mountain: Notes Toward a Wilderness Fatherhood*, and two books of poems, *Mastodon, 80% Complete* and *In the Lane We Imagined Ourselves*. His work has also appeared in various literary magazines and in *The Best American Poetry*. Johnson migrates between upper Michigan, Idaho, Scotland, and eastern Washington, where he teaches in the MFA program at Eastern Washington University.

BETH KEPHART is the author of thirteen books, including *Seeing Past Z: Nurturing the Imagination in a Fast-Forward World*; *A Slant of Sun: One Child's Courage*; *Still Love in Strange Places*; *Into the Tangle of Friendship: A Memoir of Things That Matter*; and many books for teens and children. She is the winner of numerous awards and was a Nonfiction Finalist for the National Book

Award. A graduate of the University of Pennsylvania, Kephart is currently a strategic writing partner in the award-winning marketing communications firm Fusion.

BARBARA KINGSOLVER is the author of numerous novels, short story collections, and works of nonfiction. These include *The Bean Trees; Homeland and Other Stories; Animal Dreams; Pigs in Heaven;* the best-selling *High Tide in Tucson: Essays from Now and Never; Prodigal Summer;* and *Small Wonders.* Her highly acclaimed novel *The Poisonwood Bible* was finalist for the Pulitzer and PEN/Faulkner awards. Most recently she published the nonfiction work *Animal, Vegetable, Miracle: A Year of Food Life* and the novel *The Lacuna,* winner of the Orange Prize. Kingsolver lives in southern Appalachia with her husband, Steven Hopp, and their two daughters.

ANNE LAMOTT is the author of six novels, as well as four bestselling books of nonfiction. She has taught at University of California-Davis, as well as at writing conferences across the country. Her biweekly online diary, "Word by Word," in *Salon magazine* was voted Best of the Web by *TIME* magazine. Lamott's most recent collection of essays is *Grace (Eventually): Thoughts on Faith.* Her new novel, *Imperfect Birds,* was published in Spring 2010. She lives in northern California.

BARRY LOPEZ is the author of *Arctic Dreams,* for which he received the National Book Award; *Of Wolves and Men,* a National Book Award finalist for which he received the John Burroughs and Christopher medals; and eight works of fiction, including *Light Action in the Caribbean, Field Notes,* and *Resistance.* His essays are collected in two books, *Crossing Open Ground* and *About This Life.* He contributes regularly to *Granta, The Georgia Review, Orion, Outside, The Paris Review, Manoa,* and other publications in the United States and abroad. His work has appeared in dozens of anthologies, including *Best American Essays* and *Best Spiritual*

Writing. His most recent book is *Home Ground: Language for an American Landscape*, a reader's dictionary of regional landscape terms, which he edited with Debra Gwartney.

NANCY MAIRS is a poet and an essayist. Her books include *In All the Rooms of the Yellow House; Remembering the Bone House; Ordinary Time: Cycles in Marriage, Faith, and Renewal; Plaintext: Deciphering a Woman's Life; Carnal Acts; Voice Lessons: On Becoming a (Woman) Writer; Waist-High in the World: A Life Among the Nondisabled; Troubled Guest: Life and Death Stories*; and *A Dynamic God: Living an Unconventional Catholic Faith*. She has won the 2008 Arizona Literary Treasure Award, a National Endowment for the Arts Fellowship in 1991, and the 1984 Western States Book Award in poetry for *In All the Rooms of the Yellow*. She lives with her husband, George, in Tucson, Arizona.

ROSEMARY BRAY McNATT is a Unitarian Universalist minister serving the Fourth Universalist Society in New York City. She is the author of several books, including *Martin Luther King*, a children's biography; the memoir *Unafraid of the Dark*; and *Beloved One: Prayers for Black Children*. A former editor of *The New York Times Book Review*, McNatt is a widely anthologized writer whose work has appeared in a variety of magazines and newspapers, including *The New York Times, Ms., Glamour, Essence, Redbook*, and *The Village Voice*. She is a contributing editor to *UU World*, the magazine of the Unitarian Universalist Association, and a contributing columnist for Beliefnet.com. She lives in New York City with her husband, Robert, and two sons.

JACK NISBET is a Spokane-based teacher and naturalist. He is the author of *Purple Flat Top; Singing Grass, Burning Sage; Visible Bones*; and two books about fur agent and cartographer David Thompson: *Sources of the River* and *The Mapmaker's Eye*. The Pacific Northwest Booksellers Association named Nisbet's most recent project, *The Collector: David Douglas and the Natural*

History of the Northwest, as one of their 2010 Books of the Year.

NOELLE OXENHANDLER is the author of three nonfiction books: *A Grief Out of Season*, *The Eros of Parenthood*, and *The Wishing Year*. Her essays have appeared in many national and literary magazines, including *The New Yorker*, *The New York Times Magazine*, *San Francisco Chronicle Magazine*, *Vogue*, *Tricycle*, *Parabola*, *Utne Reader*, and *O: The Oprah Magazine*. She has taught in the graduate writing program at Sarah Lawrence College and is a member of the creative writing faculty at Sonoma State University in California. A practicing Buddhist for more than thirty years, Oxenhandler is the mother of a grown daughter and lives in northern California.

GINA MIKEL PETRIE is a teacher and administrator at Eastern Washington University in the College of Arts, Letters, and Education. Gina and her husband, Greg, are the parents of five children.

LAURA READ teaches composition, literature, and creative writing courses at Spokane Falls Community College. She has published poems in a variety of journals, most recently in *The Spoon River Poetry Review*, *The New Ohio Review*, *Pank*, *The Floating Bridge Review*, and *Rattle*. Her chapbook, *The Chewbacca on Hollywood Boulevard Reminds Me of You*, was this year's winner of the Floating Bridge Chapbook Award. She lives in Spokane, Washington, with her husband, Brad, and their two sons, Benjamin and Matthew.

SCOTT RUSSELL SANDERS has published more than twenty books—novels; collections of stories; and works of personal nonfiction, including *Staying Put*, *Writing from the Center*, and *Hunting for Hope*. His latest books are *A Private History of Awe*, a coming-of-age memoir, love story, and spiritual testament, which was nominated for the Pulitzer Prize, and *A Conservationist Man-*

ifesto, his vision of a shift from a culture of consumption to a culture of caretaking.

MARJORIE SANDOR is the author of four books, including a new memoir, *The Late Interiors: A Life Under Construction*. Her most recent collection of short stories, *Portrait of My Mother, Who Posed Nude in Wartime*, won the 2004 National Jewish Book Award in Fiction. She has also published *The Night Gardener* (essays) and *A Night of Music* (stories). She teaches creative writing and literature at Oregon State University in Corvallis, Oregon.

CORA SCHENBERG has published essays in *Brain, Child: The Magazine for Thinking Mothers*; *The C'ville Weekly*; *The Hook*; and *Tough Times Companion*. She has a PhD in Germanic Languages and Literatures and teaches at the University of Virginia. She lives and writes in Virginia.

TRACY SPRINGBERRY is a Unitarian Universalist minister. She has an MA in creative nonfiction from the University of New Hampshire and an MDiv from Meadville Lombard Theological School. She has published essays in *The Sun*, *The Christian Science Monitor*, *Meadville Lombard Reader*, *Religious Humanism* and on Spokane Public Radio. She lives in Cheney, Washington, with her partner, Lisa, and four children.

JESS WALTER is the author of six books, most recently *The Financial Lives of the Poets* (2009). He was a National Book Award Finalist in 2006 for *The Zero* and won the 2005 Edgar Allan Poe Award for Best Novel for *Citizen Vince*. He lives with his family in Spokane, Washington.

BETSY WHARTON is a tumbleweed on the profession prairie. In addition to writing and raising children, she has worked as a nurse in venues as far flung as an inner-city homeless shelter, the Navajo Reservation, and a refugee camp on the Afghan border.

In her adopted hometown of Port Angeles, Washington, she has served as a small town politician and most recently she is the proprietor of the start-up food processing business known as the Clallam Canning Company. Her essay in this volume, "The Rabbi's Garage," was the winner of the 2001 AWP Intro Award and was previously published in the March 2001 issue of *Mid-American Review*.

MARION WINIK is the author of eight books of creative nonfiction and poetry, most recently *The Glen Rock Book of the Dead*. Her other works include *Telling; First Comes Love; The Lunch-Box Chronicles; Rules for the Unruly;* and *Above Us Only Sky*. Winik's essays and articles have been published in *The New York Times Magazine, O, Salon,* and *Real Simple,* among others. She writes the "Answer Lady" column for *Ladies' Home Journal,* and reviews books for *Newsday* and *The Los Angeles Times*. Winik was the recipient of a National Endowment for the Arts Fellowship in Creative Non-Fiction and has been inducted into the Texas Institute of Letters. She currently teaches writing at the University of Baltimore.

Acknowledgments

While I was in graduate school, a renowned visiting poet spoke to us about the writing craft and warned us, "If you want to be a real writer, don't have children." I thank the writers in this collection who prove him so very wrong. Thanks to my friend Tracy, the originator of this book concept. The process of compiling these essays brought unwavering focus to parenting as a spiritual path. My thanks to Mary Benard at Skinner House Books for giving this work a new and beautiful incarnation—may the book be a cherished guide for many parents. My love, always, to Doug, Nate and Jamey.

—SARAH CONOVER

I would like to thank Gina Petrie for the conversations that sparked the idea for this book. I must also thank the members of the Unitarian Universalist Church of Spokane who were so touched by the worship service Gina and I led honoring the spiritual journey of parenting that I knew telling these stories was important.

Thank you to my co-editor, Sarah, who gave this project the energy, enthusiasm, and organizational skills it needed to move forward at a time when I was tired.

This book would not have been possible without my family. My mother had complete confidence that I could do whatever I set my mind to. My children provided continual reminders on why I was editing this book and moments of quiet so I could work. My partner, Lisa, supplied unwavering love and support.

Thank you, finally, to each of the authors in this collection, who have inspired me as an editor, writer, and mother.

—TRACY SPRINGBERRY

Publication Credits

We gratefully acknowledge permission to reprint the following copyrighted works:

"2:45 P.M." from *The Lunch-Box Chronicles* by Marion Winik, copyright © 1998 by Marion Winik, and "Ashes" from *Traveling Mercies* by Anne Lamott, copyright © 1999 by Anne Lamott, used by permission of Pantheon Books, a division of Random House, Inc.; "Civil Disobedience at Breakfast" (pp. 85–99) from *High Tide in Tucson: Essays from Now or Never* by Barbara Kingsolver, copyright © 1995 by Barbara Kingsolver, reprinted by permission of HarperCollins Publishers; "Expecting Adam" from *Expecting Adam* by Martha Beck (Random House: 1999); "Life" by Alexandra Fuller, first appeared in *Granta 88: Mothers*: 2004, reprinted by permission of Melanie Jackson Agency, LLC; "Mountain Music I" from *Hunting for Hope* by Scott Russell Sanders, copyright © 1998 by Scott Russell Sanders, and "Room for One More" from *Ordinary Time* by Nancy Mairs, © 1993 by Nancy Mairs, reprinted by permission of Beacon Press, Boston; "Palsy" from *A Slant of Sun: One Child's Courage* by Beth Kephart, copyright © 1998 by Beth Kephart, used by permission of W.W. Norton & Company, Inc.; "Solomon's Blanket" from *The Night Gardener: A Search for Home* by Marjorie Sandor (The Lyons Press: 1999), reprinted by permission of Marjorie Sandor; "Boundary Loss" from *The Eros of Parenthood: Explorations in Light and Dark* by Noelle Oxenhandler (St. Martin's Press: 2001), reprinted by permission of Noelle Oxenhandler; "The Driving Lesson" from *Fathering Daughters: Reflections by Men* by Gerald Early (Beacon Press: 1998), reprinted by permission of Gerald Early; "Children in the Woods" from *Crossing Open Ground* by Barry Lopez, © 1982 by Barry Holstun Lopez (Scribner's: 1988), reprinted by permission of Barry Lopez; "The Rabbi's Garage" by Betsy Wharton from *The Mid-American Review*: Volume 22, #2, 2001, reprinted by permission of Betsy Wharton; "A Theory of Falling Bodies" by Cora Schenberg from *Brainchild Magazine*, 2001, reprinted by permission of Cora Schenberg; "Hopey Stories" reprinted by permission of Brian Doyle; "Ordinary Time" reprinted by permission of D.S. Butterworth; "The End of Summer" reprinted by permission Debra Gwartney; "Kicking and Screaming (but Going Anyway)" reprinted by permission of Gina Petrie; "Deadfall" reprinted by permission of Jack Nisbet; "Saved" reprinted by permission of Jess Walter; "At Blackhorse Lake" reprinted by permission of Jonathan Johnson; "Emmanuel" reprinted by permission of Laura Read; "The Demon's Looking Glass" reprinted by permission of Nadine Chapman; "Birthing a New World" reprinted by permission of Rosemary Bray McNatt.